JERUSALEM PRAYER TEAM
"Pray for the Peace of Jerusalem..."

www.jerusalemprayerteam.org

DR. MICHAEL D. EVANS

#1 *NEW YORK TIMES* BESTSELLING AUTHOR

MIKE EVANS

The
COMMANDED
BLESSING

TimeWorthy
BOOKS

P.O. Box 30000, Phoenix, AZ 85046

The Commanded Blessing

Copyright 2013 by Time Worthy Books
P. O. Box 30000
Phoenix, AZ 85046

Design: Lookout Design, Inc.

Hardcover ISBN: 978-1-62961-000-9
US   ISBN: 978-1-62961-001-6
Canada   ISBN: 978-1-62961-002-3

Unless otherwise indicated, all scripture quotations are taken from The New King James Version of the Bible. Copyright© 1979, 1980, 1982, 1983, 1984 by Thomas Nelson, Inc. Publishers. Used by permission.

Scripture quotations marked NIV are taken from The Holy Bible: New International Version® NIV ®. Copyright © 1973, 1978, 1984 by International Bible Society. Used by permission of Zondervan Publishing House. All rights reserved.

Scripture quotations marked NLT are taken from the New Living Translation, copyright © 1996, 2004 by Tyndale Charitable Trust. Used by permission of Tyndale House Publishers.

Scripture quotations marked ESV are taken from The Holy Bible, English Standard Version. Containing the Old and New Testaments. J. I. Packer, ed. Wheaton, Illinois: Crossway Bibles (a division of Good News Publishers), 2001.

To my beloved son,

Pastor Michael David Evans

Michael said to me, "Dad, you must write a book on The Commanded Blessing. God wants all Believers to have favor and received His commanded blessing as you have."

Michael is a mighty man of God. My wife, Carolyn, told me that God had revealed to her that the child she carried would be a son, and he would be a mighty man of God. When Michael was born, I looked at the name on his crib. It read: Michael David Evans II. I said, "Carolyn, he can't be Michael David II; I am Mike Evans and have no middle name."

I went before a judge and petitioned to have my name changed. When the judge asked why, I replied, "So I can be named after my son, and when I grow up, I can be just like him."

We now have Michael David Evans III. He has already learned to love the Lord and sings day and night. I am, indeed, enjoying the fruit of a Commanded Blessing.

PREFACE

PSALM 133–
A COMMANDED BLESSING

Through the years, numerous people have asked me, "What causes God to bless you so much?" This book is in response to that question. God is, I believe, an equal opportunity employer. He has a commanded blessing for you, as well as for me. Our responsibility is to place ourselves in a position to receive that blessing.

My father, an anti-Semite, was convinced I was not his son, but was the result of an affair between my mother, a Jewess, and a Jewish man. He strangled me and almost killed me when I was eleven. I woke up lying in a fetal position in my own dried vomit. From my earliest memories, my father had abused me. He beat me with extension cords and coat hangers so many times I would skip gym class in elementary school in an attempt to hide the marks on my back and legs. When school officials visited our home, I could not tell them the scars were the results of beatings from my father. I was certain he would kill me if I exposed him.

He would take me to the basement, hold me with one arm, and beat me with the other. Many times I wore only a pair of shorts. As he hit me with an extension cord, it would leave marks on my neck, back, legs, and arms. The pain was unimaginable.

On my way home one day, I discovered a jackknife that someone had lost in the snow. My father accused me of stealing it. "God hates liars," he screamed. "Tell me the truth! If it was in the snow, it would be rusted." I had told the truth, but it didn't stop him from making another trip with me to the basement. He shrieked, "If I have to beat you to death, you *will* tell me the truth." He punched me so hard that I wet my pants and became completely hysterical.

The only thing that saved me was that despite my panic, I lied to stop the blows; otherwise he would have killed me that night. I felt that I was cursed. The question I most often asked myself was, "Why was I born?"

My family lived in poverty in the Projects. We so often went to bed hungry that I made regular trips to the garbage dump to look for food. The rats roaming through the trash terrified me, but an old man saw me there and gave me a stick to scare the vermin away. My favorite find was what I called "white chocolate." It was actually dark chocolate with mold that grocers would throw out.

As a child, I was plagued by a speech impediment and a stomach ulcer. It is likely any social worker or sociologist would tell you that such a child would eventually end up as an alcoholic, drug addict, murdering someone or being murdered, or in prison. None of that happened. For forty-four years, I have been happily married to my best friend. We have four amazing children and nine beautiful and beloved grandchildren. I am the most blessed man imaginable.

I forgave my father unconditionally, and am the only one of the children who cared for him. My six siblings did not visit him when he was dying. Their response was, "Don't tell us he is dying; tell us when he's dead." I cared for him when he had no money. Half of each of my paychecks was sent to my parents so they could pay the house and car payments and buy food. Before my father died, he said, "Michael, I keep having a dream about black stones. My hateful grandfather, a womanizing drunk and one of the meanest people I've ever met, gave two black stones to my father. I hated him because he was just like my grandfather. My father passed the stones to me. When I tried to give them to you, you smiled and shook your head. You opened your hand, and there were two white stones. What does that mean?"

I replied, "Dad, the black stones are generational curses that were passed from grandfather to father to you. They represent curses of racism, of alcoholism, of unforgiveness, of abuse. The curses have been broken, and the white stones represent a commanded blessing—one that I will pass down to my son and grandsons. They will never know these curses."

It is my prayer that I will pass these same blessings down to you through the pages of this book. One young shepherd boy was nobody in the world's eyes. He was figuratively born on the wrong side of the tracks, and seemingly lived in a black hole—penniless and rejected. He would become one of the most prominent figures in the history of the world. He would become, perhaps, the most famous ancestor of Jesus Christ. Our Lord is often referred to as the "Son of David."

The Psalmist shared an amazing revelation in Psalm 133. In essence, he wrote that when brethren dwell together in agreement, there is power; that the place of unity is the place of power. What this book will attempt to do is to place us in harmony so that a commanded blessing can come upon you with generational curses broken.

David described the result of that commanded blessing: When we come into agreement, it releases the anointing of Aaron, the blessing of Abraham, Isaac, and Jacob, and even life forevermore—an extension to your life so that you can live fully and fulfill the purpose of God.

My dear friend, Corrie ten Boom, shared this revelation given to her by God in Ravensbruck concentration camp. She later told me that God gave her a birthday gift, Psalm 91:16, "I will reward them with a long life and give them my salvation." The significance was never fully revealed to me until Corrie died at the age of ninety-one. The Lord had given her forty years of life and ministry to impact the world for His glory.

The Psalmist not only shared this revelation, but another in Psalm 20, verses 1-6, NLT:

In times of trouble, may the LORD answer your cry. May the name of the God of Jacob keep you safe from all harm. May he send you help from his sanctuary and strengthen you from Jerusalem. May he remember all your gifts and look favorably on your burnt offerings. Interlude May he grant your heart's desires and make all your plans succeed. May we shout for joy when we hear of your victory and raise a victory banner in the name of our God. May the LORD answer all your prayers.

This prayer of David was actually a song sung by the early Church. It was a prayer for victory in times of battle. When David declared in Psalm 23:6a, NKJV, "Surely goodness and mercy shall follow me All the days of my life;" he was describing a commanded blessing that had followed him all the days of his life.

Goodness and mercy will follow you. My hope is that this prayer will be fulfilled in your life as you read this book. I do not believe it is an accident that you are reading this book; I believe one word from God can change your life forever as it has mine. May God bless you, anoint your head with oil, and may a commanded blessing rest upon you—one that will never leave.

CHAPTER 1

UNITY BRINGS BLESSINGS

Behold, how good and how pleasant it is for brethren to dwell together in unity! It is like the precious ointment upon the head, that ran down upon the beard, even Aaron's beard: that went down to the skirts of his garments; As the dew of Hermon, and as the dew that descended upon the mountains of Zion: for there the LORD commanded the blessing, even life for evermore.

(PSALM 133, KJV)

Unity and harmony was non-existent in my childhood home. Neither my parents nor my siblings dwelt "together in unity." Not until I later began to study the Word of God did I realize just how important these words are. In this Psalm, the writer paints a beautiful picture of unity in the anointing of Aaron, the high priest, brother of Moses. He pictures it being poured over Aaron's head, flowing sweetly and smoothly, fragrantly down his face, through his beard, all the way to the hem of his priestly garments. Why is that picture important? Unity is the glue that holds a family, a Church, a nation together.

In Psalm 133 David extols the value of unity. The result of such harmony is a place where God's people are refreshed and strengthened by His Spirit—just as the dew nourishes the dry ground! It is the place where God *commands* blessing and where His anointing flows! *Vine's Expository Dictionary* records that the word *together* in Psalm 133:1 "emphasizes a plurality in unity. In some contexts the connotation is on community in action."[1] And it is the place where *zoe*—Hebrew for life, the eternal, God-kind of life—flows freely!

The Hebrew word Yâchadh in verse one means "oneness, concord"; it denotes a people drawn together for one purpose—to follow Jehovah, fulfill His plan and purpose, and to dwell together under the umbrella of His blessings.

Aaron wasn't anointed with just any old oil, with whatever was handy. No; it was the holy anointing oil used only in Temple ceremonies. It consisted of four spices: myrrh, cinnamon, sweet cane (or sweet calamus), and cassia. They were mingled together with olive oil—which to the ancient Hebrews was enormously symbolic and useful. It was a balm, a soothing healing oil poured into wounds; it was fuel to keep lamps burning and provide light; it was a food—blended with grains and other foods to fill the hungry. Jeremiah asked, "Is there no balm in Gilead?" (Jeremiah 8:22, KJV.)

As the spices enfolded Aaron, it became a picture of Yâchadh—oneness—of a group of very different people united in service to Jehovah. As the oil was infused with the spices, it became holy. None of the ingredients alone could make the anointing oil, but together they become a wonderful example of unity.

When God gave Moses the list of ingredients in Exodus 30, He was very specific. He did not ask for oil and myrrh or oil and frankincense. His recipe called for four different spices—a great reminder that His Kingdom, His Church consists of "every tribe and language and people and nation" (Revelation 5:9, NIV.) These He anointed the "Body of Christ"—Christians—because we bear His name, His fragrance, His commanded blessing.

In I Peter 2:9, NKJV, Peter writes that we are a family with a purpose:

> But you *are* a chosen generation, a royal priesthood, a
> holy nation, His own special people, that you may proclaim
> the praises of Him who called you out of darkness into His
> marvelous light.

As children of God, we can rejoice for *Yĕhovah tsavah Bĕrakah*—**Jehovah commanded the blessing.**

Only when Self is subjugated to Christ will we be one with God—and each other—and have this kind of unity. We are to be one as Jesus and His Father are one. Only when Jesus is on the throne in each of our lives can we be in tune with His purpose. Only then can we be one Body on earth able to work corporately to bring true and lasting unity among the brethren. When Self is subjugated to Jesus, then His Church will flourish and grow into His fullness and carry forth His kingdom on Earth.

David paints a word picture of the refreshing this kind of harmony can bring. He likens it to the dew that nourishes Mount Hermon, a unique spot in northeastern Israel located in the Golan Heights. Once claimed by Syria, the land was reclaimed by Israel during the 1967 Six Day War. It was here on this mountain that God promised the land of Canaan to Abraham for his descendants. Long before its ownership was contested, Mount Hermon was mentioned at least a dozen times in the Old Testament—in Deuteronomy, Joshua, Psalms, and other books. It is also thought by some to be the place Matthew and Mark refer to in the New Testament as the Mount of Transfiguration.[2]

English clergyman Henry Baker Tristram wrote of the uniqueness of Mount Hermon in 1867:

> "Unlike most other mountains which gradually rise from lofty table lands and often at a distance from the sea, Hermon starts at once to the height of nearly ten thousand feet, from a platform scarcely above the sea level. This platform, to 'the upper Jordan valley, and marshes of Merom' is for the most part an impenetrable swamp of unknown depth, whence the seething vapour, under the rays of an almost tropical sun, is constantly ascending into the upper atmosphere during the day. The vapour, coming in contact with the snowy sides of the mountain, is rapidly congealed, and is precipitated in the evening in the form of a dew, the most copious we ever experienced. It penetrated everywhere, and saturated everything. The floor of our tent was soaked, our

bed was covered with it, our guns were dripping, and dew-drops hung about everywhere. No wonder that the foot of Hermon is clad with orchards and gardens of such marvelous fertility in this land of droughts."[3]

The *New Living Translation* of Psalm 133:3 says:

> Harmony is as refreshing as the dew from Mount Hermon that falls on the mountains of Zion. And there the LORD has pronounced his blessing, even life everlasting."

The commanded blessing comes through unity—in the place where peace is fostered and nurtured. David says this in his psalm; Paul admonished the Church in II Corinthians 13:11(NKJV) to "be of one mind, live in peace."

Abram (later Abraham) recognized the value and the blessings of living peacefully with others. In Genesis 13:7 (NLT) the Bible records, "So disputes broke out between the herdsmen of Abram and Lot." So great had God's blessings been upon Abram that the land could no longer contain his herds and followers together with those of Lot, his nephew, who had been blessed with an overflow of Abram's favor. The end result? Strife, confusion and chaos! It is a major arrow in our Enemy's quiver. James 3:16 (NIV) tells us: "For where you have envy and selfish ambition, there you find disorder and every evil practice."

God commands that His blessings rest on the place where there is unity and harmony. If God commands a thing, it is guaranteed; when we, as individuals or as part of the Body of Christ, "Make every effort to keep the unity of the Spirit through the bond of peace," (Ephesians 4:3, NIV.)

Abram must have been aware of God's requirements concerning unity, and in his desire for fellowship with the Creator, he said to Lot, "Let's not allow this conflict to come between us or our herdsmen. After all, we are close relatives!" (Genesis 13:8, NLT.) Because of the loving relationship between uncle and nephew, Abram allowed Lot to choose where he wanted to settle his family. This loving father-figure was more concerned with ending strife and less that he was in a land-grab.

The choices made that day were a revelation about character. Lot chose the land nearest Sodom—in the shadow of the worst possible earthly degradation and sinfulness. Abram turned from the place of strife into a God-ordained "Commanded Blessing." Upon Lot's departure, God spoke to Abram: "Go, walk through the length and breadth of the land, for I am giving it to you," (Genesis 13:17, NIV.) Everywhere his sandal struck the ground the land was to be his.

Strife and conflict can halt the flow of God's blessings. He wants, yes, He yearns for His children to leave dissension at the altar in order to pour out His benefits. Psalm 133:1 (KJV) records, "Behold, how good and how pleasant it is for brethren to dwell together in unity!" As one writer penned:

> Even if it means we have to agree to disagree, or even
> defer to another, we must declare our lives, our homes and
> our business to be "STRIFE FREE ZONES," and as we do, we
> will see and experience the "Commanded Blessings."[4]

Strife ruled in my childhood home. From the age of four, my father abused me. He broke both my arms, locked me in the canning cellar beneath our house, and once nearly succeeded in strangling me to death. I had no self-esteem—not low self-esteem, but *no* self-esteem. One Saturday my mother caught me watching Billy Graham after the morning cartoons. She walked over, snapped off the set, and warned, "Michael, Christians kill Jews, Christians hate Jews. Jesus died; don't dig Him up!" Then she sat down and told me about her grandfather, a rabbi in Minsk, Russia. On a Shabbat, he and his congregation were boarded up inside their synagogue and the building set afire. Russian Orthodox Christians on the outside screamed, "Christ killers," as the smoke spiraled heavenward. She also related that many of our relatives fled Russia to Poland and died in Auschwitz during the Holocaust.

While my mother hated Christians, my father, a professing Christian, hated Jews. "Brother Bob," as he was called, went to church regularly on Sunday morning. That was after a drinking binge on Saturday night that generally ended with him beating my mother for what he thought was her adultery. He often took his rage out on me, the end result of her suspected infidelity.

As a scared, battered eleven-year-old boy, I had a life-changing encounter with Jesus Christ. I tried one night to intervene when my father had found yet another excuse to beat my mother. He then turned his anger on me. By the time he was done using his fists on my scrawny frame, I had been dumped unconscious on the floor of my bedroom. Sometime later I awoke; every bone and joint ached. I tried to push myself up from the floor of that dark room but fell back, the room spinning.

I saw no purpose for my life. My father hated me, and my mother suffered because of me. All I knew was my father's warped version of Christianity: Booze on Friday, beatings on Saturday, and church on Sunday. My dad's favorite Bible verse must have been Proverbs 23:14: "You shall beat him with a rod, and deliver his soul from hell." He paraphrased that as "Spare the rod, spoil the child." There were no spoiled children in his home—only abused ones. He had never given me one word of affirmation. Not once had I heard "I love you" from his lips that so tenderly and lovingly caressed a glass of amber whiskey. Jack Daniels was his "friend"; I was "moron."

That night in my room, I had a life-changing encounter with Jesus Christ. As quickly as I had whispered those words, the room was flooded with a light so bright it blinded me. I thought Dad had come back to finish the job—to beat me to death, and this time I could not escape. My first thought was to crawl under the bed to protect myself. I covered my face with my hands and closed my eyes as tightly as I could squeeze them. After what seemed like an eon, I realized there was no other sound in the room. Now there was only a brilliant light. I slowly spread my fingers and eased my eyes open as imperceptibly as possible.

Instead of seeing my dad's anger-deformed face, I saw two hands reaching toward me. In the center of each wrist was an ugly scar. I had seen those scars in Sunday school literature. They were supposed to represent the nail scars of Jesus. Someone was playing a trick on me, but who? Did I dare look beyond the wrists to the face? Was I having a nervous breakdown? Was I going crazy?

Rather than the cold, stark fear that had filled the room earlier, I now actually felt warmth. I felt a Presence that brought both power and peace. I was being immersed in an invisible liquid love that poured over me and lodged deep within my soul. I slowly raised my head, and as my eyes followed the arms upward, I saw standing there in my bedroom the Lord Jesus Christ. He was either clothed in light or in the most brilliant white imaginable––whiter than fresh snow; whiter than the clouds that float in the sky; whiter than anything I had ever seen. Draped from His shoulder to His waist was a deep purple cloth––more purple than the heavens at sunset.

As I lifted my head to take in His face, I was instantly drawn to His loving eyes. They were happy eyes filled with every color of the rainbow. It was like looking into an illuminated bowl of the world's most highly prized jewels. I felt as if I could see through them and beyond to heaven and the promise of eternal peace. They were like magnets drawing me into their depths. Keeping His arms outstretched, He looked at me with an all-encompassing expression of love. He smiled and then said three things I had never heard before. They were like a healing salve to my wounded soul and spirit.

He said, "Son." It was the first time anyone had ever called me "Son." It was said so gently, with such love and respect for me––for me!––that I felt my heart melt. The word *son* echoed in my spirit again and again.

"I love you." Someone really did love me. What joy! I felt as if I'd just escaped a death sentence and was free. That statement alone was enough to sustain me for the rest of my life. But He continued, "I have a great plan for your life." The power and presence of Jesus were like a holy fire igniting my soul. I had a purpose! God had something for me to do. Then there was silence. I am sure only a few seconds had passed, but it felt like an eternity.

I closed my eyes, and tears slid slowly down my face. I was consumed with an inexplicable happiness. Eventually I realized that the light had departed but the overwhelming warmth remained. He was gone from my room but not from my spirit, not from my heart. I never wanted to lose that feeling of love and peace and warmth.

Despite my treatment by my father, as an adult and a Christian I knew I had to overcome my inner battles and make peace with him. He still exercised some power over me, and for a reason I failed to understand, his acceptance was important. No matter what I did, Dad withheld his approval. I could not get a word of affirmation from him to save my life, although I desperately wanted it. I didn't try to impress him with the people I had met or the places I had traveled. I knew that no matter what successes I might have in the ministry, he would never encourage me, never say, "I'm proud of you," never call me "son." What he did call me was "bastard" because he thought I was the result of adultery on my mother's part.

For five and a half years I sent half and more of my paycheck to help with Dad's house and car payments, yet I never heard "thank you" from him. Later in life, I continued to help with his bills and endeavored to care for him until he died.

After my father's estate was settled and I was named sole heir to his earthly possessions, I wrote a letter to my siblings in an attempt to restore family unity. It simply said:

> To my beloved brothers and sisters:
> The probate hearing is over and the judge has ruled. This is to inform you I have instructed the attorney that I will not accept the will and have withdrawn my name from it. Therefore, Dad's estate in its entirety will be divided between the six of you.
> I will absorb personal expenses incurred while assisting Dad the last few months of his life and for the funeral service. You will not be billed for anything. For years, Dad attempted to give me the estate and I refused. I wish you God's richest blessings.
> Your loving brother,
> Michael

Before my father died, I was able to forgive him. None of my siblings were able to do that. They were united by a single thread—hatred for our father. It has all but destroyed them. They have been cruel to others, violent, drug users, and more. All was blamed on their abusive childhood. Hearts and lives have been made bitter and become broken because of a refusal to seek God—because of the lack of desire to forgive. The lack of unity and harmony has all but wrecked their earthly bonds, and has certainly hindered spiritual relationships with God, the Father.

Just as this is true for families, it is true for the Church of Jesus Christ. The cry of the Father's heart is for His children to live in unity. In I Corinthians 1:10 (NIV), the apostle Paul pleads with the Church in Corinth:

> I appeal to you, brothers, in the name of our LORD Jesus Christ, that all of you agree with one another so that there may be no divisions among you and that you may be perfectly united in mind and thought.

Unity in prayer results in the commanded blessing of God. "Agreement" in Hebrew is the word *echad*; the words *"Sh'ma Yis'ra'eil Adonai Eloheinu Adonai echad."* mean "Hear, O Israel, the Lord thy God, the Lord is One." This is the first prayer every Jew learns. A united Body of Christ is like the anointing that came down from the head of Aaron to the hem of his garment. Every Believer who walks in unity receives a commanded blessing through agreement with God, and that's no small gift. The word "bless, blessed, or blessing" is mentioned in the Bible 496 times.

Everyone who has been with Christ receives God's commanded blessing. God is waiting. The angels are waiting. The kingdom is waiting. All heaven is waiting for you to be united with Jesus and to release Him in all His fullness and glory, to bless you and fulfill His destiny in you.

CHAPTER 2

OBEDIENCE BRINGS BLESSING

This day I call the heavens and the earth as witnesses against you
that I have set before you life and death, blessings and curses. Now
choose life, so that you and your children may live.

(DEUTERONOMY 30:19, NIV)

Jehovah God's blessings cannot be separated from obedience to His Word. This is never more obvious than in Deuteronomy 28: 1, 2, 15, KJV:

> ...if thou shalt hearken diligently unto the voice of the LORD thy God, to observe and to do all his commandments..., ...all these blessings shall come on thee, and overtake thee, But it shall come to pass, if thou wilt not hearken unto the voice of the LORD thy God, to observe to do all his commandments..., ...that all these curses shall come upon thee, and overtake thee."

Moses delivered this bountiful promise of Yahweh's blessings on His children if they would but obey God's commands. If they rebelled, He likewise swore the people would be cursed—cruelly cursed. Moses declared that life and blessing was in obedience to God's Word; death and destruction resided in disobedience.

How then, can you discover the blessings of God for your life? As Moses warned the Children of Israel in Deuteronomy 28:1(NIV), obedience is the key that unlocks the door to Yahweh's abundant blessings:

> If you fully obey the LORD your God and carefully follow
> all his commands I give you today, the LORD your God will
> set you high above all the nations on earth.

A loving, active, vibrant relationship with God is vital. As you live and walk daily with Him, blessings and benefits follow.

In 1978 I was invited to go with the late Jamie Buckingham, international author and columnist, on what had become for him a regular trek through the Sinai. I was looking forward to leaving my ministry cares behind to hike and fellowship with Jamie and his group of friends for eleven days, but I had no idea that God was about to teach me another important lesson of obedience. As with other paths down which God has led me, this too would be an unforgettable life experience. It seemed that God's wonderful plan for my life also included sand, heat, scorpions, and flies.

As our group followed in the footsteps of Moses, I began to draw some comparisons between his life and mine. We had both been abandoned as children—Moses out of love and a desire to be protected; me out of hatred and the abuse that followed. Eventually, Moses was rescued and protected by Pharaoh's daughter; I, too, was rescued by the assurances of Jesus that He had a great plan for my life. Even so, the feelings of worthlessness and fear that I could not have a successful ministry plagued me during the trek across the sands of the Sinai.

After returning home, I was sitting on my back steps one day when I finally reached the end of my rope. Dropping my head into my hands, I prayed, "God, my life is in Your hands. I surrender to You. If You want me to go, I'll go. If You want me to stay, I'll stay. I want only to be in Your will. You told me You loved me and had a great plan for my life. Please, Lord, speak to me again. I desperately need to hear Your voice once again."

The next day, I flew to preach for a minister friend of mine. As I sat in the confining seat in coach, I began to pray. *Lord, I have no joy, no peace. As soon as I've preached tomorrow, that's it. I'm so ashamed; I've failed You. I don't know what else to do but quit.* I turned my face to the window as tears slid down my cheeks. It was at that moment—the lowest of my ministry—that God spoke His Word into my spirit. That still, small voice said, "Isaiah 43:18–19. Pray it in faith!" I was again hearing His voice through His Word! I had no idea how big this discovery was, and that it would be as powerful as Jesus speaking to me face-to-face just as He had when I was eleven.

Then, I had no idea that the boy from the Projects would eventually claim Menachem Begin as his mentor and I would have the privilege of partnering with him to found the current Christian Zionism movement. Nor did I know that I would prophesy over a depressed twenty-eight-year-old former furniture salesman whose brother had been shot in the back in Entebbe, Uganda, during the rescue of Israeli hostages. I had no idea I would tell Benjamin Netanyahu that he would be prime minister of Israel, or that I would relate the story the following day to Prime Minister Begin, who would offer him a government position.

I reached for my Bible and opened it to read God's words of assurance:

> "Do not remember the former things, nor consider the things of old. Behold, I will do a new thing, now it shall spring forth; shall you not know it? I will even make a road in the wilderness and rivers in the desert," (Isaiah 43:18-19, NKJV.)

I had thought God was through with me; now He promised to do a new thing. I would soon find out just what it would take to see God's plan come to pass. Just as God promised to do a new thing in my life, so He began, through Moses, to do a new thing in the lives of the Children of Israel, held captive in Egypt.

You are likely familiar with the story of Moses—how his life was preserved by the quick thinking of his mother, Jacobed; how his life was saved by the daughter of Pharaoh; how he came to be reared in the household of a ruler, a house of wealth and privilege. Nothing else is recorded of Moses' life until he was a young man. But as suddenly as he disappeared from the pages of the Bible, he reappeared. Moses was out walking one day when he happened upon an Egyptian taskmaster beating a Jewish slave. So incensed was Moses that he killed the Egyptian and hid the body. The following day, he saw two Hebrew men fighting. He adopted the role of intermediary, but one of the men challenged him:

> "Who made you a prince and a judge over us? Do you intend to kill me as you killed the Egyptian?" So Moses feared and said, "Surely this thing is known!" (Exodus 2:14, NKJV.)

Immediately Moses realized that his relationship to an Egyptian princess would not spare him the wrath of Pharaoh. He had murdered a man who was carrying out a direct order from the king. Moses, having heard that Pharaoh had placed a price on his head, packed his knapsack and headed for the backside of the desert.

He was seeking a place of refuge and solitude but instead walked right into the middle of a dispute between Midianite shepherds and the seven daughters of Reuel (also known as Jethro), a Midianite priest. The men were determined to prevent the sisters from drawing water for their sheep. Moses (who probably didn't look at all like Charlton Heston) stepped into the fray, drove the shepherds away, and watered the flocks.

Three separate incidents marked Moses' early life, yet in all three he exhibited an almost compulsive need to combat wickedness. His intervention was limited to the underdog: he championed the Hebrew slave; he intervened when two Jews were fighting, and again when a group of gentiles were oppressing another like group.

Moses had no idea he would meet his future wife at the watering trough. Reuel offered Moses the job of sheepherder as well as the hand of his daughter, Zipporah, in marriage. Now Moses was content. He had a job, a wife, and soon a child, Gershom. He didn't know that he was about to face the challenge of a lifetime—greater than leaving home and family, greater than the

daily grind of taking care of the sheep. God was about to intervene in Moses'
life in a unique way.

One day as he led the sheep to the far reaches of Mount Horeb, he stum-
bled upon a bush that burned brightly but was not consumed. This was
totally against the laws of nature, and Moses turned aside to see this phe-
nomenon. He must have been stunned when from the midst of the bush the
Lord spoke to him:

> "Do not come any closer," God said. "Take off your san-
> dals, for the place where you are standing is holy ground."
> Then he said, "I am the God of your father, the God of Abra-
> ham, the God of Isaac and the God of Jacob." At this, Moses
> hid his face, because he was afraid to look at God. The LORD
> said, "I have indeed seen the misery of my people in Egypt.
> I have heard them crying out because of their slave drivers,
> and I am concerned about their suffering. So I have come
> down to rescue them from the hand of the Egyptians and
> to bring them up out of that land into a good and spacious
> land, a land flowing with milk and honey—the home of
> the Canaanites, Hittites, Amorites, Perizzites, Hivites and
> Jebusites. And now the cry of the Israelites has reached me,
> and I have seen the way the Egyptians are oppressing them.
> So now, go. I am sending you to Pharaoh to bring my people
> the Israelites out of Egypt," (Exodus 3:5–10, NIV.)

Was Moses shocked that though he had killed a man in Egypt, he was
about to be sent back to the scene of the crime with instructions to confront
Pharaoh? Now, the king from whom Moses fled had died. Moses could have
let fear rule his life, and while he did argue about his ability to sway both
Pharaoh and the Children of Israel, he ultimately chose to obey the call of
God upon his life. God had captured his attention and dealt with Moses'
concerns—he was to find his older brother, Aaron, and demand that Pharaoh
"Let my people go!"

"You shall speak all that I command you. And Aaron your brother shall tell Pharaoh to send the children of Israel out of his land…. And the Egyptians shall know that I am the LORD, when I stretch out My hand on Egypt and bring out the children of Israel from among them," (Exodus 7:2, 5, NKJV.)

In essence, God was telling Moses that his obedience would bring deliverance to the entire Hebrew nation in bondage in Egypt. Obedience would bring triumph over Pharaoh's army; submission to God would defeat the enemy. Moses and Aaron, his brother, willingly complied with God's directives; they did just as He had instructed. Together, they went before the king and demanded that he release the Children of Israel to go into the desert and worship Jehovah God.

Despite his trepidation, Moses had obeyed, and like Abraham, his obedience won him a place in the Hall of Faith in Hebrews chapter eleven, and showered the blessings of Jehovah upon his life. However, his obedience to the Creator did not end with the crossing of the Red Sea and the defeat of Pharaoh's army. Even though Moses had led the Israelites out of Egypt and into the wilderness, he had been assigned the responsibility of leading them to the Promised Land. Yet God equipped him for the task.

Moses was called by God to the heights of the mountaintop to personally receive the Ten Commandments—one of only a few to have seen God's glory and lived. He chose a young man from among the Israelites, Joshua, to accompany him halfway up the mountain. Once on the mountaintop, Moses received these instructions:

"There is a place near me where you may stand on a rock. When my glory passes by, I will put you in a cleft in the rock and cover you with my hand until I have passed by. Then I will remove my hand and you will see my back; but my face must not be seen," (Exodus 33:21–23, NIV.)

After Moses received the Ten Commandments written on stone tablets by the very finger of God, he returned to the camp to deliver them to the people waiting at the base of Mount Sinai. But what did he find when he descended out of the cloud? He found a people reveling in rebellion and delighting in disobedience. Having grown weary of Moses' absence, the Israelites had prevailed upon Aaron to make them a god of gold—a calf. "Come on," they must have said, "we don't know what has happened to Moses. We need a god that will lead us out of the wilderness." The psalmist David wrote of those who worshipped other gods. It was a description of idol worshippers of that time, but resonates with similar people of our time:

> But their idols are silver and gold, made by human hands.
> They have mouths, but cannot speak, eyes, but cannot see.
> They have ears, but cannot hear, noses, but cannot smell.
> They have hands, but cannot feel, feet, but cannot walk, nor
> can they utter a sound with their throats. Those who make
> them will be like them, and so will all who trust in them,
> (Psalm 115:4–8, NIV.)

While the people danced before the golden calf, God warned Moses of trouble in the camp, and threatened to destroy the people Moses had led out of Egypt. Moses interceded for the rebellious Israelites, and God heeded his plea to spare them. As Joshua and Moses reached the bottom of Mount Sinai, they were stunned by the sight that met their eyes:

> When Moses approached the camp and saw the calf and the
> dancing, his anger burned and he threw the tablets out of his
> hands, breaking them to pieces at the foot of the mountain.
> And he took the calf the people had made and burned it in the
> fire; then he ground it to powder, scattered it on the water and
> made the Israelites drink it, (Exodus 32:19–20, NIV.)

Moses must have turned to Aaron and demanded, "What were you thinking?!" Aaron's answer would have won an Oscar for his response and lame excuse. Can you picture him with arms upraised and a shrug of his shoulders?

"Do not be angry, my LORD," Aaron answered. "You know how prone these people are to evil. They said to me, 'Make us gods who will go before us. As for this fellow Moses who brought us up out of Egypt, we don't know what has happened to him.' So I told them, 'Whoever has any gold jewelry, take it off.' Then they gave me the gold, and I threw it into the fire, and *out came this calf!*" (Exodus 32:22-24, NIV, emphasis mine.)

Aaron didn't bow in contrition and take responsibility for his actions. He tried to justify going along with the crowd. How often does that happen—drifting into disobedience instead of taking a stand? We chuckle at Aaron's ingenuous reply, but haven't we been guilty of the same? We excuse our own behavior while pointing a finger at someone else's fall into sin.

So distraught was Moses that he literally drew a line in the sand:

So he stood at the entrance to the camp and shouted, "All of you who are on the LORD's side, come here and join me." And all the Levites gathered around him. Moses told them, "This is what the LORD, the God of Israel, says: Each of you, take your swords and go back and forth from one end of the camp to the other. Kill everyone—even your brothers, friends, and neighbors." The Levites obeyed Moses' command, and about 3,000 people died that day, (Exodus 32: 26–28, NLT.)

From the time of Adam and Eve's sin in the Garden to Christ's death on the cross, the wages of sin has always been the same: death. (Romans 6:23, KJV.) Although it must have grieved Moses to issue God's order, he was obedient, and that kind of compliance is not easy. It requires putting Self aside and clinging wholly to God's promises.

God would later call Moses to the top of the mountain to give the law again. This time Moses had to carve the stone tablets out of the rock. When he descended the mountain the second time, he didn't stop with just reading what God had dictated, he called upon the Children of Israel to be faithful to keep the laws they had been given. Moses was intent that his followers be not just hearers of the word but doers as well. As Samuel the prophet would later say to King Saul, "Obedience is better than sacrifice, and submission is better than offering the fat of rams," (I Samuel 15:22, NLT.)

> The Israelites were encouraged to obey the Word of God, to pass it on to their children:"You shall teach them diligently to your children, and shall talk of them when you sit in your house, when you walk by the way, when you lie down, and when you rise up," (Deuteronomy 6:7, NKJV.)

Moses wanted God's chosen ones to understand just what He expected from them. He wanted a people set apart from the wickedness, the depravity, and the worship of idols made by Man. They needed to specifically understand the importance of the commandments:

> "You shall have no other gods before me. You shall not make for yourself an image in the form of anything in heaven above or on the earth beneath or in the waters below. You shall not bow down to them or worship them; for I, the LORD your God, am a jealous God..." (Exodus 20:3–5a, NIV.)

During the years of wandering through the desert, Moses was obedient to the Divine instructions given him. He displayed extraordinary patience as he led a company of people that continually grumbled, complained, and mutinied. It was not surprising that eventually Moses' patience reached its breaking point, and in anger, he failed to follow God's instructions (Numbers 20). He disobeyed God at that one crucial juncture and his punishment was that he was not allowed to enter into the Promised Land. That honor would belong to his successor, Joshua. However, God *did* take Moses to the top of the mountain and allow him to see the other side—the land that flowed with milk and honey. Then Moses died and the Lord buried him. No man knows his burial site even today. (Deuteronomy 34:5–6.)

Despite missteps, Moses' life was characterized by obedience. He led a nation of rebellious, dissatisfied, disobedient, quarrelsome people through the wilderness to the banks of the Jordan River. Through all the ups and downs, the years of wandering in the desert, Moses held high the name of Jehovah-Nissi—God our banner. It was a banner of encouragement "to give you a future and a hope," (Jeremiah 29:11b, NKJV.)

Moses was able to defeat the forces of the enemy because he was submissive to God's will, and so can you. He delivered his people from the chains of darkness and degradation because he complied with Jehovah's instructions and won the unfailing commanded blessing of God.

CHAPTER 3

FAITH BRINGS BLESSING

*The L*ORD *had said to Abram, "Go from your country,*
your people and your father's household to the land I will show you.
"I will make you into a great nation, and I will bless you; I will
make your name great, and you will be a blessing. I will bless those
who bless you, and whoever curses you I will curse; and all peoples
on earth will be blessed through you."

(GENESIS 12:1-3, NIV)

According to Jewish tradition, Abram worked for his idol-worshipping father but as a young man began to doubt the value of worshipping gods made of wood and stone. He began to believe that the world had been made by one Creator. He tried to share his beliefs with his father, Terah, but to no avail. One day, in his father's absence, Abram took a hammer and smashed all the idols except the largest one. In the hands of the stone god, he placed the hammer used to wreak havoc on the smaller statues. When he was questioned by a distraught Terah, Abram replied that the largest of the statues had destroyed the others. Terah cried: "Don't be ridiculous. These idols have no life or power. They can't do anything." Abram supposedly replied, "Then why do you worship them?"[5]

One day as Abram was going about his usual activities, God called to him:

> "Go from your country, your people and your father's household to the land I will show you. I will make you into a great nation, and I will bless you; I will make your name great, and you will be a blessing. I will bless those who bless you, and whoever curses you I will curse; and all peoples on earth will be blessed through you," (Genesis 12:1–3, NIV.)

The dominant points in God's Word to Abram were that Jehovah had selected him for three central reasons: 1) to bless Abram; 2) to bless his descendants; and, 3) to bless the world through the Messiah.

It is quite easy for me to empathize with Abraham. One month after Carolyn and I were married, God gave me a scripture, and based upon His Word and the leading of the Holy Spirit, we felt directed to go to North Little Rock, Arkansas. We had received a call from Dwayne Duck, a pastor in the area. He told us about a barber, Troy Collier, who was diligently working to start a Teen Challenge Center. Troy was looking for a couple to oversee the work. When we arrived we found a table piled high with bills and a backlog of letters from people who needed a safe place to detoxify. When arrested on drug charges, offenders could choose to go to Tucker Prison, Cummings Prison, or Teen Challenge. We soon had twenty-one individuals who had committed to our program. So many young people were led to Christ that we needed a discipleship center in the countryside—away from the temptations of drug addiction and city life—to train them in the Word. Because of the faithfulness of God and His people, we soon had the facility we needed.

Aware of God's law of sowing and reaping, we planted the largest seed we had in order to begin this ministry. The outlook was bleak. There was no money, and Carolyn and I had only one room all our own the first year of our marriage, but it was a joyous, glorious year. We did everything we could possibly do for the young people God had entrusted to us. Lives were transformed.

At the end of that year in Arkansas, we moved to Chicago to begin our second work. It was there that we eventually founded our current ministry. This was the first time I would share the vision that God had placed on my heart to help the nation of Israel. The nation would become the abused mother I had always wanted to defend—and couldn't. Like Abram, I had been called to follow God's plan for my life.

Abram was living in Ur of the Chaldeans when God called him forth. Shortly after his very first conversation with the Creator, his father gathered the family together—Abram, Sarai, and Lot, his grandson—and started out for Canaan. When they reached Haran, however, the family settled. Sometime after his father's death, Abram gathered his family and crossed the Euphrates River, making their way down to Canaan.

As you read about Abram and Sarai, you see lapses in their faith, and even in their obedience. Isn't it refreshing to know that even those who are held up as examples often struggle with these issues? Old Testament men and women were as human as you and I. The truth is that God gave Abram the opportunity to learn about the benefits of submission —and he did. But not until after Abram and Sarai had been denied a child year after year; not until his nephew Lot departed and claimed the most watered area in all the land as his own, and not until Sarai grew tired of waiting on God to provide a son. Her tactics brought into the world the strife and turmoil that plagues the Middle East even today. Rabbi Matis Greenblat of *Jewish Action Magazine* wrote:

> We may be defending the most justifiable cause. And yet, the manner in which we pursue our objective is critical; so critical that if we pursue our goal too forcefully or with a measure of insensitivity the results may be disastrous.[6]

Sarai's desperate anguish over her barrenness drove her to devise a plan to provide Abram with an heir. Now, this was not God's plan. He had already promised Abram a son from whom would descend a people that numbered as many as the stars:

> But Abram said, "LORD God, what will You give me, seeing I go childless, and the heir of my house is Eliezer of

Damascus [a servant]?" Then Abram said, "Look, You have given me no offspring; indeed one born in my house is my heir!" And behold, the word of the LORD came to him, saying, "This one shall not be your heir, but one who will come from your own body shall be your heir." Then He brought him outside and said, "Look now toward heaven, and count the stars if you are able to number them." And He said to him, "So shall your descendants be," (Genesis 15:2–6, NKJV.)

Sarai couldn't wait for God to act. Now, if you've ever longed for a child, you know this desire can become all-consuming. Think of the story of Hannah, the mother of Samuel. So distraught was she as her prayers for a child were offered, the high priest thought she was drunk. The desire to hold a babe in her arms takes the foremost place in the thoughts of a woman who yearns for a child. Such was Sarai—to the point that she began to plot her own course, and that of Abram.

It was her desperation that propelled her to offer Hagar, her Egyptian handmaiden, to Abram as a surrogate. Yet, despite Sarai's interference, there is a lesson to be learned. In her misery, Sarai turned from faith in God, from dependence on Jehovah, to works—dependence on Self. She had a plan and nothing was going to deter her from seeing it come to fruition. Hagar represents works—man or, in this instance, woman—taking matters into their own hands. Abram could have said, "No." He could have reminded Sarai that God had made a promise to him and he would continue to believe God. That didn't happen. When presented with a pretty little doe-eyed handmaiden, Abram capitulated.

But, by the time Hagar was heavy with child, Sarai was consumed with jealousy and Abram was forced to endure the contentious atmosphere he had helped create within the camp. It continued to roil within him even after the babe was born and named Ishmael. And then God fulfilled His promise to Abram and Sarai. He said to Abram (loosely translated), "It's time for you to step up to the plate and walk uprightly before me. No more delayed obedience. I want your undivided attention." God then made another stipulation:

"No longer shall your name be called Abram, but your name shall be Abraham [father of a multitude]; for I have made you a father of many nations.... As for Sarai your wife, you shall not call her name Sarai, but Sarah [noblewoman] shall be her name. And I will bless her and also give you a son by her," (Genesis 17:5, 15, NKJV.)

Soon Abraham reached the age of ninety-nine and Sarah eighty-nine, both obviously well past normal childbearing age. Then came the day when Sarah awoke to find that she was pregnant in her old age. She who had laughed at the pronouncement that she would bear a child—she who had intervened and proposed her own plan for an heir—Sarah was now carrying Isaac, the son of promise. Not only had God taken away her barrenness, He provided the strength to carry the child to term and to bring it forth.

It was then that the trouble with Hagar and Ishmael became increasingly apparent. Eight days after Isaac was born, he was circumcised, and after the babe was weaned, Abraham hosted a huge celebration for the son born to Sarah. One day Sarah spied Ishmael sneering at Isaac. At that moment, her anger reached volcanic level and she exploded. Sarah demanded that Abraham literally drive Hagar and her son from the encampment with only what bread and water they could carry. Abraham had to bear the pain, heartache, and tragedy of losing Ishmael as he complied with Sarah's demands.

After God had fulfilled his vow and the child of promise had finally arrived, Abraham set about to teach God's covenant promises to his son. And then horror descended into Abraham's life:

Then [God] said, "Take now your son, your only son Isaac, whom you love, and go to the land of Moriah, and offer him there as a burnt offering on one of the mountains of which I shall tell you," (Genesis 22:2, NKJV.)

We often underestimate just how outrageous, how despicable this must have seemed to Abraham. Could this have been due in part to having grown up in a culture that condoned human sacrifice? It seems impossible to believe that he didn't question God's directive, but the narrative doesn't suggest that. (Neither is there any mention of whether he told Sarah of God's command.) You and I have read the rest of the story and know the outcome—Abraham knew only what God had demanded of him. Yet verse 3 says:

> So Abraham rose early in the morning and saddled his donkey, and took two of his young men with him, and Isaac his son; and he split the wood for the burnt offering, and arose and went to the place of which God had told him, (Genesis 22:3, NKJV.)

This time Abraham did not argue nor did he hesitate to obey God's directions. He didn't bargain with God; he didn't ask for anything in return for his obedience. Instead, he immediately made arrangements for the three-day journey to Mount Moriah. I believe his heart was so heavy it was difficult for him to place one foot in front of the other. I believe he was puzzled by God's plan. Abraham was not some Superman—a spiritual hero with mystical powers, he was "everyman" and he was about to offer his child of promise. How would you feel if you knew you were about to lose a beloved son or daughter? Abraham was surely no different.

So off they set on a three-day hike across desert terrain—a journey of some sixty miles—to the place designated by God. When they arrived, Abraham asked the servants to wait while, "the lad and I will go yonder and worship." Then he added what might well be a hint to the strength of his faith, "and we will come back to you," (Genesis 22:5, NKJV.)

After three days of spiritual wrestling with God, Abraham was assured that God would provide. As he unloaded the wood from the donkey and laid it on Isaac's back, in verse seven the lad asked, "Look, the fire and the wood, but where is the lamb for a burnt offering?" And in verse eight with great conviction and complete assurance, his father replied, "My son, God will provide for Himself a lamb for a burnt offering." Abraham had not figured out just how God would provide—a lamb wandering by, Isaac raised from the dead, a last-minute stay of execution—but he was convinced that provide God would!

I have a mental picture of father and son slowly trudging their way up the mountain to the place where God finally says, "Here; this is it." When they arrived, Abraham and Isaac set about gathering stones to erect an altar to Jehovah. Abraham carefully laid the wood and knelt before his son. He gently bound Isaac's hands and feet, and laid him on the altar. Now, Isaac was old enough to run for his life, yet he chose to stay. Not only did Abraham display deference to the will of God, so did his beloved son, Isaac.

Just as Abraham raised the knife to plunge it into Isaac's heart, an angel of the Lord cried, "STOP! Don't hurt the boy."

> And He said, "Do not lay your hand on the lad, or do anything to him; for now I know that you fear God, since you have not withheld your son, your only son, from Me," (Genesis 22:12, NKJV.)

Did Abraham hear something rustling in a bush near the altar? He looked around and there, held fast, was a ram caught by its horns. With unparalleled gratitude, Abraham untied his son, bound the ram, and laid it on the altar as a sacrifice to his faithful Jehovah-Jireh, his Provider. The angel then went one step further; he reiterated the pact God had made with Abraham:

> "By Myself I have sworn, says the LORD, because you have done this thing, and have not withheld your son, your only son—blessing I will bless you, and multiplying I will multiply your descendants as the stars of the heaven and as the sand which is on the seashore; and your descendants shall possess the gate of their enemies. In your seed all the nations of the earth shall be blessed, because you have obeyed My voice," (Genesis 22:15–18, NKJV.)

Obedience and faith go hand in hand. One cannot exist without the other. Strong faith touches the heart of God, and moves the hand of God. Obedience opens the door and releases the blessings of God, as Deuteronomy

28:2 records: "These blessings shall come upon you and overtake you." Can you imagine not being able to outrun God's abundance in your life? Being blessed simply means having the supernatural power of God at work in your life.

This extraordinary happening took place about two thousand years before Christ was born, and yet it's a perfect picture of God's offering of a substitute for our sins. He would offer up His own Son for our redemption.

Just as God was faithful to Abraham, so He is committed to His children today. He lovingly gives us just what we need—not what we want. In so doing, He fulfills His will in our lives—to redeem us unto Himself. Because Abraham obeyed Jehovah, he received perhaps the ultimate honor:

> "Abraham believed God, and it was accounted to him for righteousness." And he was called the friend of God. (James 2:23, NKJV {See also Isaiah 41:8}.)

That great orator and preacher Charles Spurgeon said of obedience:

> Having once discerned the voice of God, obey without question. If you have to stand alone and nobody will befriend you, stand alone and God will befriend you.[7]

Abraham's obedience proved to be unflinching at the command of God. Isaac, the son of sacrifice, was a foreshadow of the One who also bore the wood upon His back—His own cross (John 19:17.) Christ became the sacrifice who shed His blood for the salvation of mankind.

God had given Abram a seven-fold promise:

> I will make of you a great nation.
> I will bless thee.
> I will make thy name great.
> You will be a blessing.
> I will bless them that bless you.
> I will curse him that curses you.
> Through you all the families of the earth shall
> be blessed. (Genesis 12:2-3, paraphrased.)

God did not choose the descendants of Abram "because you were more in number than any other people, for you were the least of all peoples; but because the LORD loves you, and because He would keep the oath which He swore to your fathers..."(Deuteronomy 7:7-8, NKJV.) God will willingly and abundantly bless those who obey the edict to bless His people, Israel.

By the same token, He will curse those who curse His people. The one who speaks malevolently of you will come under the curse of Jehovah and judgment will fall. When an individual speaks vilely against Abraham and his offspring—the Chosen People—they are really attacking the Word and purpose of God, and robbing themselves of a commanded blessing.

CHAPTER 4

SUBMISSION BRINGS BLESSING

"I will do whatever you say," Ruth answered.

(RUTH 3:5, NIV)

"Submission" is a word that tends to raise the hackles of everyone—man, woman, and child. It resounds with adversarial implications for an employee who must submit to a boss, a student to a teacher, and, of course, according to biblical precepts the wife to the husband. When that word is interjected into a conversation, a sermon, a lecture, an argument, fear is often the result. Few, if any, want to be placed in a position to be exploited, dominated, manipulated, disrespected, or oppressed by another.

True submission is a choice, not something that is imposed on one, a gift that brings liberty for the giver and blessings from God when motivated by love. The Creator has given us a clear picture of submission in the life of Ruth, Naomi, and yes, even Boaz, the kinsman redeemer about whom I write later in this chapter. This Old Testament story of the woman from Moab and her devotion to her mother-in-law, Naomi, is legendary. Throughout the history of Israel Yahweh used various means to discipline His people—pestilence, drought, famine, and more.

During a period of extreme famine Elimelech, a man from Bethlehem (which means house of bread), traveled to the land of Moab with his wife, Naomi, and their two sons. Naomi's submission is evident: she was called upon to leave her home, her country, and her close relatives to follow her husband to a foreign land. Uprooting, leaving behind all you know intimately and hold dear and moving to a foreign land can incite a rampant case of culture shock. The food is different, the language is incomprehensible, and the customs unfathomable. It is not an easy passage. That is where Naomi suddenly found herself and her family—outsiders in a strange land.

It is likely that they were spurned by the inhabitants of Moab, just as the Moabites would have been in Bethlehem. What was likely to be a short relocation morphed into a span of over ten years! For ten long years they were separated from their kinsmen. The two sons, Mahlon and Chilion, took Moabite women as their wives, and it is possible that the addition of the two daughters-in-law helped to assuage some of Naomi's loneliness.

As the years passed, neither woman bore children for her husband. It was more than the disappointment of not being able to conceive for these two women; it marked the end of Elimilech's line. There would be no one to continue the family name. But nothing could have prepared her for the sword that was about to fall upon their household. First Elimelech died; Naomi was now a widow. In time, both sons died leaving her with only two daughters-in-law, Ruth and Orpah, to comfort her.

After hearing that the famine had ended, Naomi made the determination to return to Bethlehem in Judah, the land of her people. After embarking for her homeland, she halted on the way and offered emancipation to the two young women she had come to love. She encouraged them to go home to their parents, find husbands, and make new lives for themselves. To follow her meant certain hardship and isolation. Like Joshua before them, they too would have to make a life-altering decision. Having come to know Yahweh under the roof of Elimelech, they were challenged to "choose for yourselves this day whom you will serve," (Joshua 24:15, NKJV.)

Orpah, the sensible, pragmatic one finally acquiesced to Naomi's urging after much pressure and attempts to convince. Ruth refused; in her refusal she embraced Naomi's God. She turned from the darkness of paganism to the light of the God of Israel, and uttered some of the most quoted words in the Old Testament:

> "Entreat me not to leave you or to return from following you; for where you go I will go, and where you lodge I will lodge; your people shall be my people, and your God my God;" (Ruth 1:16, RSV.)

What an astounding declaration! What a mind-boggling pledge! What courageous submission! With both eyes open and well-aware of the bleak future before her, Ruth opts to devote her life to her mother-in-law—whatever may come. This is the kind of vow God wants us to make to Him, and not just to Him—to our spouses, to our children, to His people. It takes true tenacity and perseverance to go where God sends us, to live where He directs us, to love the people He asks us to love—unconditionally. Ruth made that kind of commitment to Naomi even though the journey ahead would be long, hazardous, and stressful.

Our journey to the Promised Land, like that of Ruth and Naomi, is sometimes fraught with potholes and pitfalls, with threats and travails, but the reward for submission is God's commanded blessing. We simply have to be willing to bow at His feet and say "yes" to His will.

In 1991 I underwent nine hours of intensive surgery to correct a neurological problem in my neck. For one week I endured taunting from the Enemy that God would never deign to use me again. Finally I began to pray. God's answer to the jabs from Satan was not at all what I expected to hear. I expected sympathy; I thought God would comfort me while I complained. Instead, the Spirit of God very plainly said to me, "So, the Enemy is doing exactly what he is supposed to do. It's time for you to take control of the situation."

When I asked God what He wanted me to do, I was speechless! He instructed me to go to Saudi Arabia to the staging area for the Persian Gulf War and preach the Word to the troops amassed there. Was that a suicide mission? Was He honestly asking me to submit to such a directive when it could actually mean death?

My response was typical—I think: "Excuse me, God. I had surgery a little over a week ago. You know I'm Jewish, and the Saudis don't like Jews. I'm a preacher—and they don't really like preachers, either." God simply ignored my rant.

That still, small voice whispered, "Apply for a visa."

So I grudgingly trudged down to the passport office and skeptically applied for a visa, never for one moment thinking it would be granted. One week later, and still sorely displeased by God's miraculous intervention, I set about to inform the Omniscient God of my other problem: I had no invitation, no reason to go. It wasn't like there was a Christian church on every corner clamoring for me to come preach. I didn't know a soul in that dry and forsaken country. God was surprisingly silent. It was then I knew beyond question that I had to submit to His will.

Flight arrangements were made and I climbed aboard for a twenty-plus-hour flight. When the plane finally landed, I was exhausted. After I cleared customs I went in search of a hotel. I checked in to a room, sat down on the side of the bed, and prayed, "Father, here I am. Now what?"

I opened my eyes, picked up the Saudi telephone book, and opened it randomly. I couldn't read a word of Arabic, but there before me was an advertisement with the words *Dhahran Hotel* in English. That's when God said, "Go."

A taxi took me to the hotel, and was I ever happy when I arrived! (If you've never ridden in a taxi in a Middle Eastern country, you've missed a thrill.) Over the front of the hotel fluttered a banner that read, "Joint Operation Command." Inside the hotel were also the headquarters for the various television networks each transmitting live broadcasts.

When I left my hotel room, I had tucked my Bible under my arm. I walked right into the Dhahran Hotel with it in my hand. I stopped the first official-looking person I met, stuck out my hand, and said, "How are you?"

The man looked at me with horror etched on his face. "Who are you?

And what on earth are you doing here with that Bible?" I replied that I was an evangelist from the United States.

"You're a Christian? It's impossible. How did you get here?"

"British Airlines," I smiled.

His next direction stunned me. "Go back to your hotel, pack your belongings, and be out of here within forty-eight hours. If you aren't, you will go to jail."

I began to think maybe he was right—maybe I would go to jail. Perhaps God's will was for me was to preach in prison like Paul.

After I climbed into another cab, I began to pray. I gave the taxi driver directions but had no idea where we were going. When I called out to him to stop, we sat in front of the headquarters for the 82nd Airborne stationed at the McDonald Douglas aircraft facility. I got out of the taxi, paid the driver, and walked over to the gate.

"I need to speak to the chaplain," I said to the guard.

Eventually, I was allowed to pass and given directions to the chaplain's office. His response was much like everyone else's: "I don't know how in the world you got here. What do you want?"

"I want to preach to the troops."

He shook his head in astonishment. "Well, I'll call them together, and then I'm leaving."

Submission to God's directive won me the distinct honor of preaching to our troops every day until I left the country. It was both humbling and encouraging to know that God was using me to minister to our men and women so far from home and in such precarious circumstances.

While in Saudi Arabia, the Holy Spirit spoke to me to go to Iraq to comfort the suffering refugees: *"Take food and medicine to the Kurdish people who have been targeted by Saddam Hussein."* In the middle of a field, I preached to the refugees day and night for a week. Finally my strength was gone, and I was almost too hoarse to speak. I didn't realize I was in the perfect place to be blessed by God.

Gathering all the strength I had left, I tried to think of a topic for one more meeting before my departure. All I really wanted to do was find a comfortable hotel room, take a shower, and crawl under the covers. Then I heard that still, small voice instructing me to preach my one final sermon on Jonah and Ninevah. I did the best I could, telling how Jonah rebelled against God but finally went to Ninevah. I told of the king's repentance and the revival that broke out because of Jonah's obedience. When I asked if anyone wanted to come to Christ, only one person responded—an old man in a dusty robe. I was as disappointed as Jonah had been. My interpreter was concerned about my reaction and asked, "Why aren't you rejoicing?"

"I'm happy for one soul," I said, "but I was hoping for more."

"My dear brother," the interpreter said, "the one soul who just found Jesus is the current king of Nineveh! He is the Kurdish sheik of sixteen provinces, and their capital is the site of ancient Nineveh. He has accepted Jesus and has invited you to go to Nineveh, because he believes if you will preach, they will repent."

Submission to the will and ways of God is a lesson well-learned. It brings the blessing of God into the lives of His children. Ruth had learned that lesson from Naomi during her years in Moab. That did not change the fact that she had arrived in Bethlehem with three strikes against her; she was foreign, widowed, and barren. It did not exactly put her in the running for the Jewish version of "The Bachelor." After all, who would want a woman with so many negatives? She did, however, have one positive: she had embraced Jewish law and customs. How do we know that? Ruth was willing to submit to Naomi's instructions. First, there was food to be had. Ruth had willingly assumed the role of provider for Naomi, and she needed to glean during the barley harvest. In Leviticus the Israelites were instructed:

> "When you harvest the crops of your land, do not harvest
> the grain along the edges of your fields, and do not pick up
> what the harvesters drop....Leave them for the poor and the
> foreigners living among you," (Leviticus 19:9-10.)

Ruth certainly met the criteria—she was poor, and she was an alien in the land. Her potential in Judah was non-existent, but she was willing to do whatever was necessary to care for her mother-in-law:

So she went out, entered a field and began to glean behind the harvesters. As it turned out, she was working in a field belonging to Boaz, who was from the clan of Elimelek, (Ruth 2:3.)

Her covenant with Naomi set Ruth on a course to reap a commanded blessing from Jehovah God. Had she been slack in submitting to Naomi's instructions, she would have forfeited the miraculous plan God had for her. Jeremiah 29:11 promises:

"For I know the plans I have for you," declares the LORD, "plans to prosper you and not to harm you, plans to give you hope and a future."

Just as God directed me into a danger zone in Saudi Arabia, so Naomi was prompted to send Ruth into what could have been a disastrous encounter. The omniscient Yahweh knew that Boaz was a "man of standing [Hebrew: *'ish gibbor chail,* implying Boaz was physically impressive and had noble character]."[8]

Boaz was a man of valor, a wealthy landowner, strong, honorable—a man to be trusted with Naomi's beloved daughter-in-law. Boaz might well serve as a "kinsman-redeemer"—"*go-el*" in Hebrew, a relative who could redeem a poor widow's inheritance according to Mosaic Law:

"If one of your fellow Israelites becomes poor and sells some of their property, their nearest relative is to come and redeem what they have sold," (Leviticus 25:25, NIV.)

If no one stepped forward to redeem the land, the widow was likely to live out her days destitute and distressed. Knowing that, Naomi selflessly put Ruth's future before her own. Had she been thinking only of her own future, she would have sent Ruth to the nearest kinsman, the closest, nameless, *go-el*, and not to Boaz.

Author Carolyn Custis James writes of Naomi's choice:

She wakens to the urgent need to find a safe haven for
Ruth [Ruth 3:1]…After Naomi dies, her Moabite daughter-
in-law will remain alone in Bethlehem. The thought of
this—the deeper hardship and suffering this will impose
on Ruth—is unacceptable to Naomi. She may be helpless to
prevent it, but she will at least do what she can to spare Ruth
from facing the miserable fate of a lonely foreign widow. The
only real solution in the ancient patriarchal culture is the
protection of a man. So she sends Ruth to Boaz.[9]

Knowing that she, like the widow who gave her last mite (Mark 12:43),
is offering her own future, everything, to provide one for her beloved daughter-in-law, Naomi called Ruth to her side:

"Wash, put on perfume, and get dressed in your best
clothes. Then go down to the threshing floor, but don't let
him know you are there until he has finished eating and
drinking," (Ruth 3:3.)

Was Ruth alarmed at her mother-in-law's suggestion? What terrible
thing was Naomi asking her to do? Nothing more than to follow the accepted
custom of the Jews regarding the marriage of a widow to a kinsman. Ruth
could have refused; she could have rebelled; she could have rebuffed Naomi,
yet she chose God's way—the way of submission, the way of blessing.

Naomi charged Ruth to steal onto the threshing floor, quietly uncover
Boaz's feet and lie down there. She had recently overheard Boaz reveal how
much he admired her for her dedication to Naomi, and now she was taking a chance that he might be offended and unwilling to take on the role of
kinsman-redeemer.

When Boaz awoke, he was startled to find someone at his feet:

"Who are you?" he asked. "I am your servant Ruth," she
said. "Spread the corner of your garment over me, since you
are a guardian-redeemer of our family." "The LORD bless you,

my daughter," he replied. "This kindness is greater than that which you showed earlier: You have not run after the younger men, whether rich or poor. (Ruth 3:8-10, NIV.)

Naomi sent Ruth into the night to secure her own prospects, and yet Ruth turns the tables on her cherished mother-in-law. As she has done from the beginning of the book that bears her name, Ruth resolves instead to secure Naomi's future. Her submission was not an act of gratuitous acquiescence, but an act of fortitude, purpose and resolve. Her reward: Boaz listens to her entreaty and is not offended by her presence. Ruth appeals to his integrity and his shared love for Yahweh, yet not in a manipulative or threatening way.

Knowing that the law doesn't really apply to him, Boaz refuses to turn his back on Ruth. He would submit to the Mosaic Law governing the conduct of a kinsman redeemer. Even though he was not a brother of Elimelech as the law clearly specified, but was more likely a cousin, he tells her:

> And now, my daughter, don't be afraid. I will do for you all you ask. All the people of my town know that you are a woman of noble character. Although it is true that I am a guardian-redeemer of our family, there is another who is more closely related than I. Stay here for the night, and in the morning if he wants to do his duty as your guardian-redeemer, good; let him redeem you. But if he is not willing, as surely as the LORD lives I will do it. Lie here until morning," (Ruth 3:11-13, NIV.)

The Bible does not tell us if Ruth was surprised by Boaz's announcement that there was another *go-el*, a closer relative to Elimelech whose responsibility it was to provide covering for Naomi. He assured Ruth, however, that he had a plan and would not let the coming morning pass before he had approached the other kinsman. As the sun crept near the horizon, Boaz arose, poured out six measures of barley, tied it up in Ruth's veil and sent her on her way back to Naomi.

Ruth Chapter 4 reveals Boaz's persistence in claiming her as his wife. Following the letter of the law could have meant that Ruth was claimed by another. Even though he could legally have walked away, Boaz willingly chose to take on the responsibility of Naomi and Ruth. At first light, he traveled into town to the city gate, the seat of all legal transactions. He encountered Mr. Nameless Relative, and drew him and ten elders aside for a business conference. Boaz related the story of Naomi and Elimelech, reminding the kinsman of his responsibility to redeem the land. At first eager to purchase the property, Mr. Relative balked when confronted with the other shoe that is about to drop:

> Then Boaz told him, "Of course, your purchase of the land from Naomi also requires that you marry Ruth, the Moabite widow. That way she can have children who will carry on her husband's name and keep the land in the family," (Ruth 4:5, NLT.)

Marry Ruth? Wait just a minute! Mr. Nameless Relative needed a moment to weigh the matter. Marriage to the Moabitess woman would create a problem with his sons, causing them to lose a portion of their inheritance. The acquisition of Elimilech's land was not worth the risk; the cost was too great:

> At this, the guardian-redeemer said, "Then I cannot redeem it because I might endanger my own estate. You redeem it yourself. I cannot do it," (Ruth 4:6, NIV.)

Awarded the right to redeem the land, Boaz submitted himself, his possessions, and his future into the hands of Yahweh and became an ancestor to the true Kinsman-Redeemer, Jesus Christ. The once childless Ruth miraculously gave birth to a son, Obed, who was the grandfather of King David of the lineage of Jesus. Ruth chose submission; she chose life; she chose to be both obedient and courageous, and became an ancestor of the Messiah (Matthew 1.)

Because of their submission to the will and way of Jehovah, Naomi, Ruth, and Boaz each discovered *hesed*, the "consistent, ever-faithful, relentless, constantly-pursuing, lavish, extravagant, unrestrained, furious love." [10] They chose Jehovah's commanded blessing.

CHAPTER 5

REPENTENCE &
RESTITUTION BRING
BLESSINGS

But before they were born, before they had done anything good or
bad, she received a message from God....She was told, "Your older
*son will serve your younger son."**

(ROMANS 9:11A, 12, NLT)

One of the lessons the Old Testament account of Jacob and Esau
has to offer is that of repentance and restitution, and the blessings that follow. It could be said that those two boys were born fighting.
They struggled in their mother Rebekah's womb, and when born, Jacob's
tiny hand grasped Esau's heel. So, the boys were named—Esau, meaning
"hairy" because he was born covered with red hair; and Jacob, meaning
"he who supplants" or usurps another's place.

The Bible tells us little of their childhood other than that Esau grew
to be a hunter and Jacob a dweller in tents. There is one other important
detail about their lives that plays an important role in the story of the two
brothers:

> Isaac loved Esau because he enjoyed eating the wild
> game Esau brought home, but Rebekah loved Jacob. (Gen-
> esis 25:28, NLT.)

Perhaps it was Isaac's and Rebecca's very acts of partiality—favoring one son over the other—that fostered the spirit of rivalry, contention, and bitterness between the twins. Like the discord between Isaac and Ishmael, it created a feud that has lasted nearly four thousand years.

Esau was the elder, by minutes probably, the child charged with carrying on the family business. Instead he was *ish-sadeh* which is translated "a man of the open fields." He was a man who shirked his responsibilities for the joy and thrill of hunting. Esau was impulsive, headstrong, disobedient, and hedonistic—he thought first of his own desires and their fulfillment instead of home and hearth. Jacob, though often thought of as wily and deceptive, was *ish-tam* which translates to "a man who ultimately went wholeheartedly after God."

After a long day of hunting, Esau arrived home to the smell of a pot of lentil stew hanging over Jacob's fire. Esau's first thought was of his own belly. "I'm starving to death," he might have cried. "Jacob, give me some of your stew."

Jacob offered to exchange a bowl of soup for his brother's birthright—the exclusive right of the oldest son to a double portion of his father's wealth. Esau apparently had no qualms about trading his inheritance for a bowl of beans and quickly devoured the meal. Just as swiftly as his hunger was satiated, he apparently forgot about the deal with his brother.

Isaac, aware that he was near death, knew it was time to impart blessings upon his sons. He called Esau to his tent and asked him to kill a dear and make the savory stew that he loved. Isaac promised that after he had eaten, he would bestow a blessing upon Esau. Rebecca overheard Isaac's plan to bless Esau as his firstborn and began to plot how she could advance the promise God had given her before the birth of her sons:

> "Two nations are in your womb, and two peoples from
> within you will be separated; one people will be stronger

than the other, and the older [Esau] will serve the younger [Jacob]," (Genesis 25:23, NIV.)

Rebecca then hatched a scheme to deceive Isaac. She explained the ruse to Jacob, and he eagerly jumped onboard.

A nineteenth century English preacher, Frederick W. Robertson, delivered a memorable treatise entitled, "Isaac Blessing His Sons." During the sermon he turned to Genesis 27:9-13 and read the words of Rebecca to Jacob:

> "Go out to the flock and bring me two choice young goats, so I can prepare some tasty food for your father, just the way he likes it. Then take it to your father to eat, so that he may give you his blessing before he dies.... Let the curse fall on me. Just do what I say" (Genesis 27:9-13, NIV.)

Robertson explained that even the most passionate human devotion, if unprincipled, will not bless but destroy. Said Robertson:

> "Here we see the idolatry of Rebekah; sacrificing her husband, her elder son, her principle, her own soul, for an idolized person. Do not mistake. No one ever loved child, brother, sister, too much. It is not the intensity of affection, but its interference with truth and duty, that makes it idolatry.
>
> "Rebekah loved her son more than truth, that is, more than God.... The only true affection is that which is subordinate to [God's higher authority].... Compare, for instance, Rebekah's love for Jacob with that of Abraham for his son Isaac.
>
> "Abraham was ready to sacrifice his son to duty. Rebekah sacrificed truth and duty to her son. Which loved a son most? Which was the nobler love?"[11]

Rebecca dressed Jacob in his brother's smelly clothing in order to fool his nearly-blind father into believing he was Esau. Was Isaac actually fooled by the trickery? Perhaps—perhaps not. He did, however, bestow the double portion belonging to the eldest son upon Jacob:

> "May many nations become your servants, and may they bow down to you. May you be the master over your brothers, and may your mother's sons bow down to you. All who curse you will be cursed, and all who bless you will be blessed," (Genesis 27:29, NLT.)

When Esau found out what had happened, he was understandably livid:

> Esau hated Jacob because their father had given Jacob the blessing. And Esau began to scheme: "I will soon be mourning my father's death. Then I will kill my brother, Jacob," (Genesis 27:41, NLT.)

Esau went to his father, bowed before him and pleaded for a blessing. With a heavy heart, Isaac responded:

> "Your dwelling will be away from the earth's richness, away from the dew of heaven above. You will live by the sword and you will serve your brother. But when you grow restless, you will throw his yoke from off your neck," (Genesis 27:39-40, NIV.)

Simply stated, the words were less a blessing, more a curse. While Jacob would enjoy God's commanded blessings, Esau and his descendants would make their home in an arid land, live under the threat of constant battles, and be servants to Jacob except for rare periods of rebellion. Esau's spirit was crushed and his anger overwhelming.

Knowing that Esau was exceedingly angry with Jacob, Isaac again called for his youngest son and gave yet another blessing—the covenant inheritance and blessings of Abraham:

"May God Almighty bless you, And make you fruitful and multiply you, That you may be an assembly of peoples; And give you the blessing of Abraham, to you and your descendants with you, that you may inherit the land in which you are a stranger, which God gave to Abraham," (Genesis 28:3-4, NKJV.)

Jacob fled Canaan and eventually arrived at the city of Luz. It was there that God visited him in a dream and repeated the same promises He had make to Abraham and Isaac. Jehovah then personally pledged His blessing and protection to Jacob (Genesis 28:10-15.) Jacob was so overjoyed that he renamed the city Beth-el which means "House of God," (verse 19.)

Jacob eventually arrived at the home of his mother's brother, Laban, who would teach the young man the true meaning of "deceitful." He deceived Jacob into first marrying Leah, the eldest daughter, before allowing him to marry Rachel whom Jacob loved. Even so, God fulfilled His promise by blessing Jacob with abundant herds.

It would be years before Jacob returned home. While working for Laban, Jacob sired twelve sons and one daughter, and became a very wealthy man. The day finally came when Jacob was so homesick he gathered his family and flocks, folded his tents and set out for Canaan. As they neared the land, Jacob sent word to his brother, Esau that he was coming home. When the messengers returned, their news was disturbing:

"We came to your brother Esau, and he also is coming to meet you, and four hundred men are with him." So Jacob was greatly afraid and distressed, (Genesis 32:6-7, NKJV.)

As you might imagine, Jacob's knees must have knocked together in fear. It didn't look good for the brother who had deceived his twin out of a blessing. Four hundred men—were they coming to greet him, or to destroy him and his family? He divided his large entourage into two camps, and then did the only thing left to do—he fell on his face before Jehovah God in prayer and supplication:

"O God of my father Abraham, God of my father Isaac,
O LORD, who said to me, 'Go back to your country and your
relatives, and I will make you prosper,' I am unworthy of all
the kindness and faithfulness you have shown your servant.
I had only my staff when I crossed this Jordan, but now I
have become two groups. Save me, I pray, from the hand of
my brother Esau, for I am afraid he will come and attack me,
and also the mothers with their children. But you have said,
'I will surely make you prosper and will make your descendants like the sand of the sea, which cannot be counted,'"
(Genesis 32:9-12, NKJV.)

Alone in the camp, on his face before God, Jacob was attacked. He must
have been terrified thinking that it was one of Esau's men come to kill him.
All night, Jacob wrestled for his very life. As the light of dawn peeked over
the horizon, Jacob realized that this was no ordinary foe; somehow he knew
he was wrestling with an angel of God. In order to end the combat, his
opponent touched Jacob's hip socket and dislocated it. The Divine wrestler
shouted, "Let go of me!" Jacob refused:

"I will not let you go unless you bless me." The man asked
him, "What is your name?" "Jacob," he answered. Then the
man said, "Your name will no longer be Jacob [ambitious
deceiver], but Israel [the prince who prevailed with God],
because you have struggled with God and with men and
have overcome." Jacob said, "Please tell me your name." But
his foe replied, "Why do you ask my name?" Then he blessed
him there. So Jacob called the place Peniel, saying, "It is
because I saw God face to face, and yet my life was spared."
The sun rose above him as he passed Peniel, and he was
limping because of his hip, (Genesis 32:26-31, NKJV.)

God had been convinced that Jacob, now Israel, was single-minded in
his resolve to hold on to Jehovah even though he had been injured. With

the injury, Jacob could no longer fight Esau in hand-to-hand combat. He was now the prey, totally dependent on God's mercy and Esau's grace. Jacob had been promised blessings by God; would he also be shown mercy by his brother?

Over the horizon, Jacob could see the men who accompanied his brother. He watched as a man separated himself from the rest of the company and began to walk toward him. Suddenly, the man broke into a run. It was Esau:

> But Esau ran to meet Jacob and embraced him; he threw
> his arms around his neck and kissed him. And they wept,
> (Genesis 33:4, NKJV.)

Esau, who could have harbored hatred and resentment toward his brother, offered forgiveness to a repentant Jacob. God's blessings are poured out when repentance and restitution are practiced. And yet, despite his forgiving Jacob, the New Testament refers to Esau in Hebrews 12:16 (KJV) as "profane"—a word originally used for an area outside the tabernacle that held no sacred purpose. Esau lived an earthly, secular life focused only on the present—the now. He apparently had no close relationship with Yahweh. While he had forgiven Jacob, Esau and his brother were strangers spiritually. Jacob returned to Yahweh, to Beth-el, and Esau continued to live a life separated from the blessings of God.

Forgiving someone who has wronged you is one of the great challenges of life. Those who harbor unforgiveness are burdened with misery and guilt. Those who refuse to forgive overflow with rage and resentment. Their hostility is a wall that encloses them, and no one can scale that wall. Unforgiveness may go unnoticed by the individual to whom it is directed, but it defiles the one who bears it. It can, and sometimes does, literally destroy the body and the soul of the one bearing the ill-will, and it certainly blocks the flow of God's blessings into that life.

Releasing unforgiveness is not something one does easily. The normal reaction is to either retaliate or hold on to resentment. Forgiveness flies in the face of every natural instinct. The sad truth is that when you harbor unforgiveness—against a spouse, parent, co-worker, or anyone who wronged you—it separates you from God and His bounty, and that person controls your life. God has called you to forgive which sets you free from sin and death, from the past, and from separation from God. It allows you to enjoy exceedingly abundant blessings.

The story of Jacob and Esau is one of family forgiveness; however, there are times when that forgiveness must be offered to our extended church family. One Sunday morning at church, a man approached me and introduced himself. His name was Ray. After we had chatted for a few minutes Ray, who seemed like a very godly man, said the Lord had impressed him to ask me for help. He needed to borrow $32,500 for one week. He offered to give me a post-dated check, which I was to deposit at the specified time. Wanting to help a brother in need and not taking time to pray about it, I agreed to help him. The next day Ray accompanied me to the bank, where I secured a cashier's check in the amount he needed. In turn, he handed me the post-dated check. Ray skipped town with our money and left me holding a worthless piece of paper.

I was devastated! Jesus kept admonishing me to "forgive ... forgive." After several weeks of hearing the same message from above, I snapped, "Easy for You to say 'forgive!' He didn't rip off Your $32,500! It was mine!" The moment I said this, I realized my ignorance. God had given His Son for me—and for that man. Everything I had was His. I fell on my knees in the bedroom and prayed, "I forgive Ray, Lord. Help him to make things right with You."

I felt strongly that because I had forgiven Ray, our nest egg would be returned. A scripture in Proverbs flooded my spirit: "Yet when he [the thief] is found, he must restore sevenfold." That night I wrote the word "Return" on a piece of paper. As I held it up before God, I felt impressed to write a book and call it *The Return*. Within ninety days the book was a reality and in the next twelve months became a bestseller. The royalty from sales was exactly seven times what had been stolen from us! Forgiveness opened the door for a commanded blessing in my life.

CHAPTER 6

FORGIVENESS & MERCY BRING BLESSINGS

Moreover He called for a famine in the land;
He destroyed all the provision of bread. He sent a man
before them— Joseph—who was sold as a slave.

(PSALM 105:16-17, NKJV)

It was October 1991, the conclusion of Operation Desert Storm, the first Gulf War. Israel was again being forced to the bargaining table, and I was on my way to Madrid for the Madrid Peace Conference. The site for the various meetings in the days to come was the richly appointed royal palace. But the beautiful interior was all glitter and no substance, a disguise for its actual purpose: the place where even more land-for-peace would be demanded of the Jews.

During one of the meetings, I prayed silently as I gazed at the ceiling in the grand Hall of Columns. It was ornately embellished with the images of false gods: Apollo, Aurora, Zephyrus, Ceres, Bacchus, Diana, Pan and Galatea. From their lofty perch, these bogus gods looked down on the official proceedings to elicit a counterfeit peace. Like the apostle Paul at Mars Hill, I found myself praying to the one true God while under this canopy of idolatry. How ironic that Israel had been forced here, of all places, for

an international peace conference—to Spain, where one-third of the Jewish
population of its day had been massacred during the Inquisition. I watched
sadly as representatives of nation after nation mounted the podium to insult
and accuse Israel, and to demand that her leaders relinquish the majority of
her land.

I can still hear their voices reverberating through the marble halls: "We
will accept your land in exchange for peace." What they were really saying
was: "This is a stick-up. Give me all your land and you won't get hurt—
much." I tend to think of muggings happening on the streets of major cities, yet the Madrid Peace Conference, by any measure, was an international
mugging. And the world was the silent witness too intimidated to report it
to the police. Most of the nations represented pretended not to see the "gun"
pointed at Israel's head.

As I left one of the meetings, the Syrian foreign minister stopped me. He
pulled a picture of Yitzhak Shamir from his pocket and told me he intended
to accuse the prime minister of being a terrorist while he was a member
of the *Irgun* (an early Israeli paramilitary organization). I borrowed a cell
phone and called Benjamin Netanyahu to relate to him what I had been told.
The next morning before the beginning of Shabbat and in the presence of
President George H.W. Bush, President Gorbachev, and other world leaders,
Mr. Shamir stood and said, "I have to leave now. I am an Orthodox Jew, and
I leave these proceedings to my able delegation." Thirty minutes after he
departed, the Syrian foreign minister stood to speak but faced only an empty
chair where Shamir had sat.

The blessings of God rested on me as I found myself virtually in every
session in the royal palace. To my knowledge I was the only minister of the
Gospel present for the majority of the Middle East Peace Conference.

At the conclusion of one session, the Egyptian foreign minister and
the Syrian secretary of state came up to me and asked if I was a minister. I
looked the Egyptian foreign minister in the eye and asked, "Will you obey
the words of your most distinguished prime minister and secretary of state?"

He was puzzled. "We have never had a person who was both prime minister and secretary of state. If we had such a man, I would certainly obey his words."

I related the story of Joseph in the Old Testament where he had forgiven his brothers for having him imprisoned. "Joseph was prime minister and secretary of state of Egypt and embraced his brothers. Will you do the same?"

Much like the meetings in Madrid, the saga of Joseph and his half-brothers opened with jealousy, hatred, callousness, and misery. The plot was filled with anxiety, fear, and confusion.

As the account begins, Joseph, Jacob's son by his beloved Rachel had grown into a young man of seventeen. To his discredit, he flaunted his father's partiality in the faces of his older siblings. To add fuel to the fire of discontent, Jacob had presented Joseph with a beautiful coat woven with cloth of many colors. Each of his sons had a knee-length, sleeveless tunic—plain and functional—but Joseph's coat was something special. It was not merely utilitarian; it was colorful, ankle length, and bore long sleeves. It was a symbol of a father's love for a special son, and the brothers despised both father and son because of the favoritism.

At this juncture, Joseph was not the wise elder statesman that he later became, and tact was apparently not his strong suit. He had dreams from God, and rather than ponder them in his heart, shamelessly shared their contents with his disgruntled brothers. Two of Joseph's dreams depicted him as a ruler to whom his brothers must bow down. Really, now! The others were outraged with Joseph's impudence, and even his father scolded him:

> "What is this dream you had? Will your mother and I and
> your brothers actually come and bow down to the ground
> before you?" (Genesis 37:10, NIV.)

His father's rebuke failed to stop Joseph from being insolent. Finally the brothers had had enough of his cheekiness. Ten of his siblings—Asher, Dan, Gad, Issachar, Judah, Levi, Naphtali, Reuben, Simeon, and Zebulon— connived to rid themselves of Joseph. They saw their chance when Jacob dispatched Joseph to Shechem to inquire about the well-being of his sons who were tending the flocks. As they saw him in the distance, their first plan was to simply kill him. When Joseph arrived at the camp, the brothers grabbed him, tore his coat from him, and tossed him into a pit. Reuben, not wanting to murder his own brother, pleaded with the others to spare Joseph's life. Spotting a caravan of Ishmaelite traders on its way to Egypt, Judah suggested they sell him as a slave. They then pulled Joseph from the hole in the ground and sold their brother. They may have thought he would perish en route or would be worked to death after he arrived—but God had other plans for that brash young man.

As the procession continued on its way across the desert, the brothers plotted to explain his son's absence to Jacob. They killed a young goat and sprinkled its blood on Joseph's colorful coat. Jacob's partiality had so hardened their hearts that they apparently had no difficulty in presenting the offending garment to their father and insinuating that Joseph had been killed. Jacob was inconsolable—he who had once deceived his own brother was now deceived by his sons. What irony!

The Bible doesn't say explicitly, but somewhere between Shechem and Egypt, Joseph must have gained some spiritual maturity. Once in the land of Pharaoh, he was sold to one of the king's military leaders, Potiphar. When the general's wife tried to seduce Joseph, he fled her presence. We are told that hell has no fury like a woman scorned, and Potiphar's wife was no exception. She contrived to have Joseph put in prison. Perhaps he wondered how his dream of being a ruler would ever come to pass in his trek from pit to prison. He may have thought he had reached his final destination and would perish in chains, but:

> The LORD was with [Joseph]; He showed him kindness and granted him favor in the eyes of the prison warden. So the warden put Joseph in charge of all those held in the prison, and he was made responsible for all that was done there. The warden paid no attention to anything under Joseph's care, because the LORD was with Joseph and gave him success in whatever he did, (Genesis 39:21-23, KJV.)

When two of his prison mates—the king's baker and butler—had dreams, Joseph was able, with God's help, to interpret them. After three days, the butler was restored to his position of trust, but the baker was beheaded for his perceived crime. One night Pharaoh had a very disturbing dream. The butler, remembering Joseph's gift for interpretation, told the king about the young man he had met in prison. Joseph was summoned from his cell to the palace. His journey from pit, to prison, to palace had been long and arduous, but Joseph was about to reap the blessings of having lived a life of integrity in Egypt.

As Joseph stood before the king, God gave him the interpretation of the dream: seven years of miraculous abundance followed by seven years of harsh austerity. So impressed was Pharaoh with Joseph that he immediately appointed him prime minister and placed him in charge of the country's agricultural program over the following fourteen years. During the feast years, Joseph preserved much of the grain in vast storehouses across the land. When famine hit the land, Joseph set regulations to disburse the grain in a manner that would safeguard the lives of the Egyptians and their surrounding neighbors.

As scarcity gripped the land of Canaan, Jacob was told that there was plenty of grain in Egypt. God was setting the stage for one of the most poignant examples of mercy in the Old Testament. Jacob sent his ten eldest sons to the land of Pharaoh to purchase grain:

> Now Joseph was governor over the land; and it was he
> who sold to all the people of the land. And Joseph's brothers
> came and *bowed down before him with their faces to the earth,*
> (Genesis 42:6, NKJV—Emphasis mine.)

Joseph's dream was realized—and his brothers did not even recognize him. He began a prolonged game of cat-and-mouse. Joseph presented test after test that lasted over a period of months, and possibly years, in order to determine if his brothers were still the hateful, scheming siblings that had sold him into slavery. He was not being vindictive as we will see, but rather viewed what his brothers meant for evil as part of God's plan to save his family. In the final challenge, Joseph demanded that the youngest brother, Benjamin, be brought to Egypt the next time the clan returned for grain. Jacob refused to allow him to go until the time came that they must either buy grain or perish, but relented after his son Judah assured Benjamin's safety.

In this final test, Joseph tried to ascertain if the brothers would abandon Benjamin as they had abandoned him. Was he being unforgiving? No, he was simply trying to determine if his brothers had become more caring individuals. When the time came for the men to return to Canaan, Joseph had his steward divide the funds used to buy the grain and place a portion in each man's sack. In Benjamin's sack, Joseph instructed that the steward was to also place a silver chalice. The men had not gone far from the city when the steward with a contingent of soldiers apprehended them and accused them of stealing from the prime minister's house. Feeling they were being unjustly blamed, the brothers vowed that anyone caught in possession of stolen property would become the prime minister's (Joseph) slave.

The grain sacks were opened and Joseph's cup was discovered in Benjamin's possession. The brothers were stunned. Judah approached Joseph and said:

> "Your servant my father said to us, 'You know that my wife bore me two sons. One of them went away from me, and I said, he has surely been torn to pieces. And I have not seen him since. If you take this one from me too and harm comes to him, you will bring my gray head down to the grave in misery.' So now, if the boy is not with us when I go back to your servant my father, and if my father, whose life is closely bound up with the boy's life, sees that the boy isn't there, he will die. Your servants will bring the gray head of our father down to the grave in sorrow. Your servant guaranteed the boy's safety to my father. I said, 'If I do not bring him back to you, I will bear the blame before you, my father, all my life!' Now then, please let your servant remain here as my LORD's slave in place of the boy, and let the boy return with

his brothers. How can I go back to my father if the boy is not with me? No! Do not let me see the misery that would come on my father," (Genesis 44:7-34, NIV.)

Joseph could no longer control his emotions. He cried to his steward to have the room cleared. The brothers' reunion would be held in private, not before the Egyptian servants. As soon as the last Egyptian left the hall, Joseph revealed his identity to his brothers. They were even more terrified to discover that the brother they had threatened to kill and then sold into slavery stood before them. Not only was Joseph their sibling, he now possessed the power to retaliate a hundred fold, but instead of chastising them, he cried:

"I am Joseph! Is my father still living?" But his brothers were not able to answer him, because they were terrified at his presence. Then Joseph said to his brothers, "Come close to me." When they had done so, he said, "I am your brother Joseph, the one you sold into Egypt! And now, do not be distressed and do not be angry with yourselves for selling me here, because it was to save lives that God sent me ahead of you. For two years now there has been famine in the land, and for the next five years there will be no plowing and reaping. But God sent me ahead of you to preserve for you a remnant on earth and to save your lives by a great deliverance. So then, it was not you who sent me here, but God. He made me father to Pharaoh, LORD of his entire household and ruler of all Egypt," (Genesis 45:3-8, NIV.)

Can you imagine the fear that must have gripped his brothers? They had been wary enough of the powerful Egyptian official standing before them; now, they discovered it was Joseph, their own brother whom they had betrayed. The brothers must have felt their likelihood of any leniency had evaporated. Their only prayer was for mercy. As the blood drained from their faces in fear, guilt stripped them of all hope and left them standing in abject silence before Joseph. In the first fifteen verses of Genesis chapter 45, the brothers spoke not one word. They stood, I imagine with heads bowed, until they were certain of Joseph's intentions.

Joseph did not minimize what had been done to him or the consequences, but he assured his siblings that he recognized there had been a purpose for the path his life had taken. God had been in control of his darkest nights and his brightest days. The capacity to bless those who had wronged him was because he had experienced the commanded blessing of a gracious God upon his life. Forgiveness for Joseph was not without cost. He had paid the price for his brothers' jealousy; he had spent years in exile from his father; he had suffered at the hands of others. However, he chose to forgive. True forgiveness is a decision of the heart, and Joseph willingly made that choice. Joseph was able to love those who had spitefully used him because of Jehovah's grace and mercy displayed toward him.

God had not halted the flow of blessings in Joseph's life when he was reunited with his brothers. He sent a caravan to transport his father, brothers, and their families to Egypt. Can you picture the reunion? Joseph is waiting impatiently to see his father when the word comes that his family is approaching the city. Joseph orders his chariot to be brought around, eagerly climbs inside, and strikes out to meet them. His driver reins in the racing horses as Joseph bounds to the ground before the wheels stop turning. He races toward his father and throws his arms around him, and his brothers watch—jealousy a thing of the past, forgiveness extended and embraced, and Jehovah's blessings flow abundantly.

Despite hatred, hardships, pits, prisons, and famine, God's plan had prevailed. The seed of Jacob, once thought dead, lived and thrived in the fertile soil of the Nile. God's promise to Abraham in Genesis 32:12 would be fulfilled.

As you read the story of Joseph, you realize that Joseph forgave his brothers pro-actively; they were forgiven before they ever set foot inside the palace. He took the initiative because Joseph understood that God had elevated him in order to save his family. You may see that as a real challenge—pro-active forgiveness. Perhaps you think that forgiveness should only be extended when the one who has wronged you grovels for pardon. No, the answer is in mercy—even if it is never sought. By canceling the debt and extending grace you are giving yourself a gift that money cannot buy. And, it frees God to work in the life of the person who has harmed you. You are also moving closer to becoming the person God wants you to be. He wants to free you from anger and release your emotional ties to a hurtful past in order bless you abundantly.

CHAPTER 7

HUMILITY BRINGS BLESSING

Elijah was a human being, even as we are. He prayed earnestly
that it would not rain, and it did not rain on the land for
three and a half years. Again he prayed, and the heavens gave rain,
and the earth produced its crops.

(JAMES 5:17-18, NIV)

There are times in a man's life when he must come face-to-face with his enemy and trust solely in God to see him through the encounter. Elijah was such a man, an intrepid individual in biblical history. It is he who confronted King Ahab, whose wife, Jezebel, imported the worship of the idol Baal from Phoenicia. As Elijah performed his duties as a prophet of God, the day came when, despite all the miracles he had performed at God's bidding, he was told his assignment would be handed to another. But before we assign Elijah to a fiery chariot and the balcony of heaven, let's review his life as a humble prophet who first appears on the scene in I Kings 17:1:

> And Elijah the Tishbite, of the inhabitants of Gilead, said to Ahab, "As the LORD God of Israel lives, before whom I stand, there shall not be dew or rain these years, except at my word."

Now that's definitely out of left field! Elijah gets right in the king's face and says, "Hey, Ahab, no rain—not even dew for the next three years. God said so!" Needless to say, his popularity with Ahab and Jezebel plummeted.

All we know about Elijah at this point is that he was an inhabitant of Tishbeh (reputedly in the Upper Galilee region.) Some Bible scholars think he had migrated from there to Gilead. It was, as we say in Texas, "out in the boondocks." Before Elijah, whose name means "my God is the Lord" burst on the scene, the northern kingdom, Israel, had been ruled by a succession of wicked men. When we first meet Elijah, Ahab had ascended to the throne after the death of his father Omri. The Bible says he had "done worse than all that were before him," and that was bad! Ahab entered into an arranged marriage with Jezebel, the daughter of King Ethbaal, a Phoenician. (I Kings 16:31, KJV.) The kingdom had come under the thumb of Ahab and his queen, Jezebel, and that, according to Charles Swindoll, was "a little like going from Jesse James to Bonnie and Clyde,"[12] or from the frying pan into the fires of hell.

Some historians record that Jezebel's parents were a high priest and priestess who worshipped Baal (one of the seven princes of hell.) She, too, was likely a priestess. For the first time in the books of Kings and Chronicles, we are introduced to the wife of a king of either Judah or Israel. There is, therefore, some biblical significance associated with Jezebel. It is for a very good reason that her name has come to mean an impudent, shameless, or morally unrestrained woman.[13] She was a ruthless and pagan queen, a thief and a murderess.

Ahab was apparently what we today would call a "henpecked husband," one who resorted to pouting and grumbling to get his own way. He frequently acquiesced to Jezebel's wishes and leadership in ruling the kingdom. He apparently knew that if he wanted something badly enough, Jezebel would make it happen. In I Kings 16, we begin to see why God called Elijah as a prophet to Israel:

> He [Ahab] set up an altar for Baal in the temple of Baal
> that he built in Samaria. Ahab also made an Asherah pole
> [a sacred tree to honor the pagan goddess Asherah] and did

more to arouse the anger of the Lord, the God of Israel, than
did all the kings of Israel before him, (I Kings 16:32-33, NIV.)

Ahab had not been the first king over the northern kingdom to promote
idol worship. His ancestor, Jeroboam, was the first to plant the seeds of idolatry in the region:

> Jeroboam did not change his evil ways, but once more
> appointed priests for the high places from all sorts of people.
> Anyone who wanted to become a priest he consecrated for
> the high places, (I Kings 13:33, NIV.)

The term "high places" was used to describe the pagan altars where the
Israelites worshipped idols of wood and stone, and where they sacrificed
their children to the gods of the Canaanites. The murderous and deceptive
Jeroboam laid the foundation for his successors, including Ahab. This is the
atmosphere into which Elijah would be sent to proclaim the Word of God.

First, God commanded Elijah to go to the Brook Cherith where he
would have water during the terrible drought that had gripped both Israel
and Judah. God promised to supply the prophet with food delivered daily
by ravens. The big, black birds are omnivorous, meaning they dine on both
plant and animal matter. How many would be humble enough to eat what the
ravens dropped on the driveway daily? Yet Elijah trusted God and depended
on Him for survival.

Faith? Yes! Humility? Definitely! The man or woman of God obeys
whether in the glare of the spotlight or hidden in a cave by a stream; whether
eating filet mignon or bird food. Elijah placed his very life in God's hands.
He submitted to the command immediately without question or hesitation.
When the drought worsened and the brook dried up, it was time for Elijah to
trust his future to Jehovah. Perhaps the prophet had felt the urging from God
to step out in faith and move to a new location. No matter the reason for the
move, Elijah was about to find out that wherever he was sent, a commanded
blessing awaited the obedient servant of Yahweh.

God sent the prophet in a very specific direction—on a long, dangerous trek from his cave all the way to the Mediterranean coast. His destination was Zarephath; his next place of safety, the home of a widow and her only son. Elijah asked her for bread and water. Her answer must have stunned the prophet:

> "As surely as the LORD your God lives," she replied, "I don't have any bread—only a handful of flour in a jar and a little olive oil in a jug. I am gathering a few sticks to take home and make a meal for myself and my son, that we may eat it—and die," (I Kings 17:12, NIV.)

Jehovah breathed the solution into Elijah's spirit:

> "Don't be afraid. Go home and do as you have said. But first make a small loaf of bread for me from what you have and bring it to me, and then make something for yourself and your son," (I Kings 17:13, NIV.)

That instruction must have been humbling—the great prophet of God sent to eat a piece of flatbread from the last smidgen of flour and oil the widow possessed. Elijah was not to give; he was to take. As a prophet of God accustomed to the miraculous, he surely must have wanted to be the one to provide an abundant supply for this widow—a room filled with oil, flour, lentils, vegetables—but no. Like the Children of Israel who received manna sufficient for the day, God supplied a daily quantity of flour and oil for the widow, her son, and her houseguest. She had trusted God for provision; Jehovah-Jireh, the God who provides, answered.

Because the widow offered Elijah the last of her food, God miraculously supplied her needs:

> The bin of flour was not used up, nor did the jar of oil run dry, according to the word of the LORD which He spoke by Elijah, (I Kings 17:16, NIV.)

Corrie ten Boom, long esteemed by evangelical Christians as the ideal of Christian faith in action, was confined to the Ravensbruck concentration camp with her sister, Betsie who suffered from pernicious anemia (a chronic blood disease.) Before being transported to the camp, a friend had given Corrie a bottle of liquid vitamins. As the desperate days mounted, Corrie found that she was more often forced to share her hoard of the life-giving liquid rather than save it solely for Betsie. Corrie was stunned when she realized that though she often administered the precious drops to as many as twenty-five women in a day, the contents never ran dry. She was reminded of the woman in the Old Testament, the widow of Zarephath, whose cruise of oil held a perpetual supply as long as there was need of it — all because she willingly gave all that she had to the prophet Elijah.

One day one of the nurses from the infirmary smuggled a bottle of the precious liquid to Corrie. She rejoiced to be able to refill her small bottle. God's provision was truly confirmed that night as she held her bottle upside down to drain the last drop. No matter how long she held it or how many times she tapped the bottom, the bottle refused to give up another single drop. As God provided the new, the old ran dry.

During his stay in Zarephath Elijah would have an opportunity to repay the widow a thousandfold. Her child died. She desperately needed a miracle, so this distraught mother lifted the still little body and carried her son to the prophet. Elijah took the boy. There was no wailing, no gnashing of teeth, and no questioning of God's power or ability. She trusted God's supernatural power to do what she could not; He had proved faithful to meet not only the prophet's needs, but those of her and her son. Elijah didn't chide the grieving mother. He responded with kindness. This heartbroken mother had no idea of the miracle that was about to take place:

> "Give me your son," Elijah replied. He took him from her arms, carried him to the upper room where he was staying, and laid him on his bed. Then he cried out to the Lord, "Lord my God, have you brought tragedy even on this widow I am staying with, by causing her son to die?" Then he stretched himself out on the boy three times and cried

out to the Lord, "Lord my God, let this boy's life return to him!" The Lord heard Elijah's cry, and the boy's life returned to him, and he lived. Elijah picked up the child and carried him down from the room into the house. He gave him to his mother and said, "Look, your son is alive!" Then the woman said to Elijah, "Now I know that you are a man of God and that the word of the Lord from your mouth is the truth," (I Kings 17:19-24, NIV.)

It is interesting to note that Elijah "stretched himself out on the boy three times." The number three in Scripture represents resurrection. Jonah spent three days and nights in the belly of the whale. The Apostle Paul crouched in the darkness, eyes blinded, for three days. Our Messiah lay in a borrowed tomb for three despairing days and nights before He burst to life.

God commanded a resurrection blessing in the life of the boy. Elijah turned to Jehovah-Rophi, the God who heals, and He answered. Elijah was able to present the young child, in perfect health, to his grieving mother! His boldness, obedience, and willingness to follow direction had positioned Elijah for God's commanded blessing upon his life and ministry.

For nearly three years, Elijah hid from Ahab and Jezebel, first by the brook and then in Zarephath. Why? Because the queen had spent those three years diligently trying to annihilate the prophets of God. She had succeeded in killing all but 101—Elijah and one hundred prophets hidden in caves by Obadiah, Ahab's palace administrator, who fed them from his own food supply. In actuality, Ahab was unknowingly feeding the very men Jezebel was determined to slaughter.

Suddenly, God told Elijah it was time for him to make his presence known to Ahab and Jezebel. As he went on his way, he met Obadiah who ironically was out with Ahab "looking" for the hidden prophets. Elijah's first words were, "Take me to Ahab." Obadiah was stunned—not to mention in fear for his life. He was concerned that if he went to tell Ahab Elijah had surfaced, then "as soon as I leave you, the Spirit of the Lord will carry you away to who knows where. When Ahab comes and cannot find you, he will kill me," (I Kings 18:12, NLT.)

Elijah assured the king's administrator that he would hold his ground until he saw Ahab:

> "I swear by the LORD Almighty, in whose presence I stand, that I will present myself to Ahab this very day." So Obadiah went to tell Ahab that Elijah had come, and Ahab went out to meet Elijah. When Ahab saw him, he exclaimed, "So, is it really you, you troublemaker of Israel?" (I Kings 18:15-17, NIV.)

Standing before the king was a tired, dusty, humble man—a picture of both heroism and humility—waiting to deliver God's message. Ahab had not seen his nemesis for three years, during which time the country was gripped by drought and famine. On his trek from the widow's modest dwelling to the royal palace, Elijah must have encountered the dead and the dying. He must have been confronted with hopelessness at every turn, but he knew that God was about to move, the situation about to change. El Elyon, the Most High God, had a plan, and no king, no evil dictator, no worldly queen, or circumstances could foil His plans or change His mind.

Into the presence of the earthly ruler of Israel walked the man deemed responsible for the whole problem—Elijah. Ahab tried to lay the blame at the feet of the prophet, but the humble prophet was not alarmed. He simply turned the tables on the king and leveled the charge:

> "You and your family are the troublemakers, for you have refused to obey the commands of the LORD and have worshipped the images of Baal instead," (I Kings 18:18, NLT.)

Ahab had shamelessly flaunted the first two commandments and had not only placed Baal before Jehovah; he had set up groves in honor of the deity. According to author Matt Barber:

> The principal pillars of Baalism were child sacrifice, sexual immorality (both heterosexual and homosexual) and

pantheism (reverence of creation over the Creator). Ritual-istic Baal worship, in sum, looked a little like this: Adults would gather around the altar of Baal. Infants would then be burned alive as a sacrificial offering to the deity. Amid horrific screams and the stench of charred human flesh, con-gregants—men and women alike—would engage in bisexual orgies. This ritual of convenience was intended to produce economic prosperity by prompting Baal to bring rain for the fertility of "mother earth."[14]

The United States today is following the same path, but it is strewn with politically correct words such as "same-sex marriage," or "pro-choice." The terrible truth is that our children are being sacrificed on the altar of Self to the god of "Me."

Elijah boldly stood before Ahab and said something like, "Hey king, you can't blame me for this mess. It's all your fault! You made the choice to dis-obey God's laws. If you want to know why we haven't had rain, Ahab, look in the mirror. It is *you* who has forsaken Yahweh to go after false gods."

The prophet's next directive was a call to action:

"Now summon all Israel to join me at Mount Carmel, along with the 450 prophets of Baal and the 400 prophets of Asherah who are supported by Jezebel," (I Kings 18:19, NLT.)

The call went out and the crowd gathered. Elijah had his instructions from God and was ready to face the 850 false prophets. Of course, he had the advantage: he knew the winner before the first side of beef hit the altar of Baal. However, he had a point to prove to a vacillating nation. He defined the question:

"How much longer will you waver, hobbling between two opinions? If the LORD is God, follow Him! But if Baal is God, then follow him!" (I Kings 18:21, NLT.)

Too often meekness and humility are equated with weakness. Not true of Moses, and certainly not true of Elijah! He unwaveringly faced an indecisive congregation. God had anointed him for that time and place, for that day and hour. When the flames died, he would exhibit incontrovertible evidence that Jehovah alone was the one true God.

The priests of Baal presented their offerings to their god. With much dancing and shouting, they tried vainly to call down fire from heaven to consume the gift. Standing over to the side, leaning on a pile of stones that had once been an altar to Jehovah, Elijah chided the worshippers of Baal and Asherah:

> "Shout louder!" he said. "Surely he is a god! Perhaps he is
> deep in thought, or busy, or traveling. Maybe he is sleeping
> and must be awakened," (I Kings 18:27, NIV.)

The activity around the altar to Baal only grew more frenzied. The priests jumped about like a pile of frogs just released from a gunny sack. They howled like long-tailed cats in a room full of rocking chairs. They cut themselves until blood ran down their arms—and their god remained silent. It was absolute bedlam, total idiocy. All day, Elijah watched as the priests and prophets of Baal descended into hysteria followed by incapacitating exhaustion. Finally, they dropped into the dust surrounding the altar—bloody, spent, and disgraced.

At last, God's time had come. Elijah gathered twelve stones, one each to represent the twelve tribes. He then erected an altar to Jehovah. Not satisfied, he dug a trench around the structure deep enough to hold approximately 50 pounds of wheat. He arranged layers of wood on top of which he laid the offering. Then he said:

> "Fill four large jars with water and pour it on the offering
> and on the wood. Do it again," he said, and they did it again.
> "Do it a third time," he ordered, and they did it the third
> time. The water ran down around the altar and even filled
> the trench, (I Kings 18:33-35, NIV.)

After the offering and the wood were soaked and the trench was filled with water, Elijah prayed a twenty-four word prayer:

> "Answer me, LORD, answer me, so these people will know
> that You, LORD, are God, and that You are turning their hearts
> back again," (I Kings 18:37, NIV.)

No fanfare. No shouting. No frenzy. No self-mutilation. Just a quiet, confident trust in the God of Israel. Suddenly, without warning, fire fell from heaven, consumed the offering, the wood, the stones, the soil beneath the stones, and the water in the trenches! The Children of Israel fell on their faces before God and acknowledged His sovereignty.

Elijah had undergone the ultimate in character-building exercises. He had been called out of hiding to stand toe-to-toe with an angry king and his dangerous and vindictive queen. He had been asked to exercise superhuman faith in the God of the Hebrews. He faced down 850 frantic, feverish, and frenzied false prophets—and God commanded a supernatural blessing because of Elijah's unwavering trust.

The prophet had walked in lock-step with Jehovah from the brook Cherith, to Zeraphath, through miraculous provision and healing. He was assured that God would take care of him.

Elijah's showdown on top of Mount Carmel is reminiscent of another showdown on top of Mount Calvary. Each was a battle between light and darkness, a battle between good and evil, a challenge between Jehovah and Satan. Elijah was a man of great faith and humility; Jesus Christ was the epitome of faith and humility. No wonder His disciples responded, "Elijah," when Jesus asked, "Who do men say that I, the Son of Man, am?" (Matthew 16:13, NIV.)

Near the top of any list of truly humble men would surely be the name "Elijah." The prophet's life is a prototype of Christ before His journey to the cross. The comparisons are many: both were humble, tender, kind, and patient. Yet upon occasion, both uttered scorching words of judgment and retribution. Elijah learned the lessons of humility during a devastating famine in the land. Is there a famine in your land today? Perhaps it is a financial famine, and the job that provided food and drink has dried up. How are you thinking about your circumstances? Consider that God is your source—He is the One who can meet your every need, daily. He knows what you have need of and how to provide for you, His child.

Is your famine found in a crumbling relationship that you thought would endure "until death do us part?" Your hope is fading; your tears soak your pillow at night. Is it time to return with Elijah to Zerephath? If we could interview Elijah today, he would certainly assure that it was Jehovah's lesson in obedience and humility that prepared him for the challenge atop Mount Carmel. As you meditate on the life of Elijah and his walk of faith, look heavenward to the Author and Finisher of your faith for the grace to walk humbly before Him.

Just as Elijah was challenged to face down his enemy, Ahab, I, too, was directed to stand before Yasser Arafat—another very dangerous man—and challenge him. When I was thirteen, I had circled a scripture in my Bible:

> "Fear thou not; for I [am] with thee: be not dismayed; for I [am] thy God: I will strengthen thee; yea, I will help thee; yea, I will uphold thee with the right hand of my righteousness. Behold, all they that were incensed against thee shall be ashamed and confounded: they shall be as nothing; and they that strive with thee shall perish," (Isaiah 41:10-12, KJV.)

The words of that passage were especially comforting when I heard that Ronald Reagan had refused to allow Arafat, the pistol-waving terrorist, to attend the General Assembly in New York, and because of that restriction the United Nations would convene a special session in Geneva, Switzerland. The voice of God spoke to my spirit through that scripture as clearly as He had spoken to me audibly when I was eleven.

I flew to Geneva on December 9, and checked into the Hilton Hotel, all the time believing that somehow God would cause me to ride upon the high places of the earth. He would open doors to leaders of nations because I was delighting in Him. I knew if it came to pass, truly supernatural affirmation from the Father would come with it.

To my amazement, I was allowed into the facility where the General Assembly meetings were being held, but would only be allowed upstairs in the nosebleed section. During the breaks I shared the Gospel with dozens of ambassadors and foreign ministers. After Arafat had delivered his speech, it was concluded that he had not clearly stated that he would denounce terrorism as expected. He was then forced to hold a press conference, which was predominantly peopled by the executive council and members of the PLO. The location had not been divulged to the general public.

The moment I heard of the meeting, I walked the halls of the building in prayer. The Spirit of God spoke to me and directed me to go to room 401. Once inside, He sent me to the second row of seats next to a long table. There I was instructed to put my locked briefcase on the center chair and then leave the room.

Hours later, Arafat's cronies filled the room where strict security was in place to keep out those who were unwanted. When the room was completely filled, I approached one of the terrorists guarding the door.

"Excuse me, sir, I need to go to my seat."

"You have no seat here. You cannot enter," he snapped.

"But I have already been inside," I said. "Go to the front row of chairs. You will see my briefcase on the second row, middle seat. Open it; the combination is 0001. Inside you will see my passport and several other things."

He turned and stalked up the aisle. Shortly he came back and reluctantly escorted me to the chair that held my briefcase. Minutes later, Arafat arrived. I was directly in front of him in the middle seat. The camera crews had been assigned row three—just behind me. Not even the PLO executive council had been permitted to sit in rows one and two. The cameramen were protesting because my head was in the way.

Before me was a table where Arafat and the few men who accompanied him were to sit. They entered the room, and the PLO chairman delivered his speech.

After his speech, he said, "I shall allow three of you to speak. You may choose among yourselves."

I knew they would not choose me, so I instantly grabbed my Bible and stood to my feet secure in the scripture that God had activated in my life. In my other hand was a copy of the PLO covenant, which calls for the destruction of the State of Israel.

I said, "Mr. Arafat, if you denounce terrorism you must condemn this covenant that calls for the destruction of Israel." Then, while holding up my Bible, I began to recount the biblical position of the Jewish people.

When I finished speaking, I turned; not only was Arafat livid, but I was surrounded by men whose eyes were filled with murderous hatred because of what I had said. I prayed: *Lord, You divided the sea for Moses. I only need about twelve inches to get out of this room.* Suddenly it was as if a carpet had been rolled out. I saw a path I could navigate, and walked quickly through the midst of the gathering into the dark hallway. The voice of the Enemy taunted me with "You'll never make it out of here alive. They will stab you in the back." I had no idea where I was going but went in the direction I felt prompted by the Spirit to go. *"A cab will be waiting with the door open,"* the Lord directed: *"Get in and go to your hotel. No man will harm you."*

It happened exactly as the Spirit of God had indicated. In just minutes, I was safely inside my hotel room in Geneva, offering praise for my life.

In Micah 6:8 (NLT) the prophet reveals more of Jehovah's criteria for His commanded blessings:

> ...this is what he requires of you: to do what is right, to
> love mercy, and to walk humbly with your God.

Humility and obedience will bring you into a place of receiving a commanded blessing. Or as Oral Roberts was fond of saying, it puts you "under the spout where the glory comes out."[15]

CHAPTER 8

SURRENDER BRINGS BLESSING

Submit yourselves, then, to God.

(JAMES 4:7, NIV)

My wife, Carolyn, and I are the proud parents of three beautiful daughters. In 1984 God gave us a fourth gift—a son. Carolyn said to me, "Honey, I want to name him Michael David Evans II after you." There was only one problem with that: I reminded her that I didn't have a middle name.

Her smiling response was, "Well, that's your problem."

My next stop was the courthouse where I had my name legally changed to Michael David Evans. When the judge asked me why I wanted to do that, I told him I wanted to be named after my son.

Now Michael and I share the middle name of one of Israel's greatest kings: David. We are blessed because King David is a perfect example of all four components necessary to activate God's commanded blessing.

In I Chronicles, the second chapter, the lineage of David is preserved for posterity. The chronicler wrote: "And Boaz begat Obed, and Obed begat Jesse." David was Jesse's youngest son, the runt of the litter, the sheepherder. Samuel was the high priest in Jesse's day. It was a rare thing for the man who held that position to be out in the field searching for a candidate to be king. Saul had been king, and yet God had rejected him because of disobedience. Not only did God reject Saul, He repented of having chosen him to rule over His people, Israel. Now He had sent Samuel on a mission to find the man who would be king:

> The LORD said to Samuel, "How long will you grieve over Saul, since I have rejected him from being king over Israel? Fill your horn with oil, and go. I will send you to Jesse the Bethlehemite, for I have provided for myself a king among his sons," (I Samuel 16:1, ESV.)

Samuel was dispatched to the house of Jesse to anoint one of his several sons. As each stood before the high priest, Jesse wondered: Would it be the tall, handsome one? Would it be the most skillful one? Would it be the son considered to be a warrior?

It is likely that Samuel looked at Eliab and was reminded of Saul, the king with such promise. I Samuel 9:2 records that Saul was "a head taller than any of the others." Unfortunately, stature had not produced a competent king, nor did it qualify Eliab to wear the crown.

As Jesse's sons paraded before him, surely Samuel would know which one was the right man; but as Jesse watched silently, he realized none would do. God rejected each of them for the role of king. He did not reject the man—no, not at all! Each one was beloved by God. It was simply that Jesse's older boys were not God's choice to rule over Israel: I Samuel 16, verse 10 notes, Jesse tried to present each son to Samuel in his best light, but without success. Finally, a disappointed Samuel said to Jesse, "The Lord has not chosen these. Is that all?"

Jesse thought of his youngest son who was out in the field keeping the sheep. He was certain he had known which of his sons would be the choice to become king, but there was no one left—except the youngster.

Jesse must have reasoned: "He's just a kid. He lives alone—well, just him and the sheep. How in the world could he be God's choice? He's not qualified. Surely Samuel doesn't intend to anoint David! He's just my harp-playing, psalm-singing son, occupied with sticks and stones and a slingshot. He just watches the sheep—a woman's job." But Jesse obeyed Samuel and sent someone to fetch David. Samuel was determined that the gathering would not eat until the last son had stood before him and God.

David was stunned when someone showed up to take his place in the sheepfold. He had been called home with no preparation, no indication of what the problem might be. Maybe he stopped by a stream to wash the smell of the sheep off his hands. Perhaps he just ran straight home; we don't know. What we do know is that the moment Samuel saw this handsome young man with the beautiful eyes, he said, "He is the one! I will anoint him." Just as Jesus said years later, "The last shall be first," (Matthew 19:30, KJV.)

Regardless of what Jesse or Samuel thought, God had chosen David. He had equipped His choice in the Judean foothills; He had seen the heart of a servant in David; and He had watched as the young shepherd developed skills to protect his father's flocks that had been entrusted to him. Now the youngest was to become king:

> Then Samuel took the horn of oil and anointed him [David] in the midst of his brothers; and the Spirit of The LORD came upon David from that day forward, (I Samuel 16:13, NKJV.)

As Jesse's offspring, David was to be a key ancestor of Jesus Christ:

> There shall come forth a shoot from the stump of Jesse, and a branch shall grow out of his roots.... In that day the root of Jesse shall stand as an ensign to the peoples; him shall the nations seek, and his dwellings shall be glorious, (Isaiah 11:1,10 RSV.)

Indeed, God looked deeply into David's heart and saw a man who was thankful, who would admit his sin (unlike Saul) and repent wholeheartedly; a man who had absolute faith in Jehovah, and who loved God's Word. He was a man committed to doing God's will and following His precepts. (See also Acts 13:22.)

From the day of Samuel's visit to Jesse's house, David's life would never be the same. When he was called home from his duties as a shepherd, he could have hesitated. Yet he walked confidently onto the scene, obedient to the prophet, to his father, and to his God. David took his place at the forefront of Jewish history, and on the throne that would one day be occupied by the Messiah.

David then spent years of his life running from King Saul, the man he was anointed to replace. He was rejected by the one whom he served as armor bearer. He was ridiculed by his brothers, and in Psalm 27, David says, "[Even] my father and mother forsake me," (Psalm 27:10, NIV.) Perhaps you, like me, have been rejected by a mother or father, a sibling, or a beloved child. We can learn one valuable lesson from David: Rejection does not determine our anointing—only God can! Rejection does not strangle the flow of God's blessings in the life of a Believer.

This man after God's own heart willingly served his father as a shepherd. It had not been his lot to be the eldest with the greatest inheritance, or the warrior who served under the king. No, it was his job to rise early in the morning to tend the sheep, to spend lonely days and nights finding food and water for his charges, protecting them from marauders that attacked. It was his place to submit to the will of his father, Jesse, to follow his instructions, even if it meant being the laughingstock of his siblings.

I can empathize with David. In my own life, after Jesus appeared to me when I was eleven, I kept it to myself. Dad would have thought I was lying, and that always meant a beating. Mom would have been horrified that I had given my life to Jesus. I didn't tell my brothers and sisters because I knew I would be mocked and criticized.

After David was anointed by Samuel, there came a morning when Jesse ordered his youngest son to take supplies to his brothers who were battling the Philistines in the Valley of Elah. Upon his arrival, David saw the imposing figure of Goliath and heard the challenge being hurled across the valley to his quaking audience on the other side. David was incensed that no one in

Saul's army had the courage to face the giant. They all stood on the sidelines, intimidated by the ferocity of the huge warrior. But David was not foolhardy; he knew beyond a doubt that only through the power of God could anyone defeat this adversary. He asked those around him what would be the reward for the one who slayed the enemy. David's brothers were angered by his question and began to ridicule him. He then marched before Saul and offered to fight the giant.

When Saul questioned both his youth and ability, David replied:

> "I have been taking care of my father's sheep and goats.... When a lion or a bear comes to steal a lamb from the flock, I go after it with a club and rescue the lamb from its mouth. If the animal turns on me, I catch it by the jaw and club it to death. I have done this to both lions and bears, and I'll do it to this pagan Philistine, too, for he has defied the armies of the living God! The LORD who rescued me from the claws of the lion and the bear will rescue me from this Philistine!" (I Samuel 17:34–37, NLT.)

David was a man of great humility; he knew that he was unable to do anything except through the power of God. He declined to accept any commendation for his feats; he gave God the credit. He boldly assured Saul that God would stand with the man who dared go forth in His name; God would give him the victory. In humility, David offered himself as an instrument in his Father's hands.

King Saul offered David his personal armor for the battle with Goliath. After having tried it on, the young man realized that the covering made by mortal hands was insufficient for the task. Like the apostle Paul, David understood he was only safe when covered with the full armor of God. He would be vulnerable in Saul's armor; he would be invincible wrapped in the presence of Jehovah-Sabaoth—the Lord our Protector.

In this modern-day "me first" society, instead of doing it God's way, we've done it our way. James 1:17 (NKJV) says, "Every good gift and every perfect gift is from above, and comes down from the Father of lights..." We need to acknowledge God's provision and offer the praise due Him. He is the Source of every good thing—life, health, opportunity, talent, and blessing. God is Jehovah-Jireh, our Provider.

David learned that lesson as a shepherd. God had miraculously provided protection for him and his flock. When he faced the giant, he was prepared. Crossing the brook, David selected five smooth stones and dropped them in his shepherd's bag. As he approached the valley of Elah, Goliath began to fling insults:

> He said to David, "Am I a dog, that you come at me with sticks?" And the Philistine cursed David by his gods. "Come here," he said, "and I'll give your flesh to the birds and the wild animals!" (I Samuel 17:43-44, NIV.)

David's battle cry was simply, "I come against you in the name of the Lord Almighty, the God of the armies of Israel, whom you have defied," (I Samuel 17:45b, NIV.)

God had proven to be strong in battle, present during trials, a Light in the darkness, springs of Living Water in the desert, David's Provider. That was the basis for his humility, knowing that he himself could do nothing, but that he could do anything through God if his faith was rooted and grounded in Him. It identified David as a wise leader, not an egotistical power monger.

In the end, Goliath lay on the ground—a stone embedded deeply in his forehead. David used the giant's own weapon to lop off his head and give Israel the victory—not by might, nor by power, but by the Spirit of the Lord of hosts, (Zechariah 4:6, paraphrased.) David had long known that with God on his side, he was in the majority.

From David we learn that operating in humility does not mean renouncing your own self-esteem. While some would view a humble man or woman as a submissive doormat, the truth is that through God the individual possesses power—controlled by strength and self-control.

When his brothers belittled him in front of the entire army of Israel, David forgave them. When his father didn't think him worthy to be introduced to Samuel, David forgave him. David spent his early years running and hiding from Saul. He was stalked like a criminal because of Saul's jealousy. David hid in caves, took refuge in enemy territory, rejected opportunities to kill his adversary, and loved Saul's son, Jonathan.

The future king had become the hunted outlaw with a price on his head. Day and night for years Saul dogged David, just waiting for the moment when David would become vulnerable. The desire of Saul's heart was to plunge his spear through the man he deemed his adversary.

Jealousy turns giants into jerks! Saul had a golden opportunity to demonstrate greatness when the Israelites sang, "Saul has slain his thousands, and David his ten thousands." (1 Samuel 18:7, NKJV) Saul could have taken a bow for sending David into battle. He would have only become bigger in the eyes of the people. Instead, he became bitter.

Success sometimes causes people to turn on you with a jealous rage. When that happens, know this: What God has told you in secret will keep you from giving up in the greatest battles of your life. Get your eyes off what you're *going through*...and get them on what you are *going to*—God's commanded blessing!

Soaked with sweat, betrayed and embattled, lonely and weary, David took refuge in the cave of Adullum:

> "And every one that was in distress, and every one that was in debt, and every one that was discontented, gathered themselves unto him; and he became a captain over them: and there were with him about four hundred men," (1 Samuel 22:2, KJV.)

There was no self-promotion for David. He was isolated in a wintry cavern. Things were going from bad to worse, but David refused to become a victim of "cave mentality." He was surrounded by the distressed (those under pressure or stress), by debtors (people who could not pay their bills), and by the discontent (those bitter of soul). Did he fall into self-pity? Not David! He turned a curse into a blessing by gathering those men around him and teaching them how to become mighty men of valor!

Have you ever found yourself in a pit of despair—distressed, in debt, and discontented—hoping against hope that someone would come around and point you in the right direction? Step out of the darkness into the brilliant light of God's Word! Abandon the pity party for a praise-party.

It was not God's will for David to surrender to the pressure of the chase! David was destined for the throne. He was in the cave, but the cave was not in him! David was content to wait on God's commanded blessing—for Jehovah to elevate him to a place of honor. So David, the anointed shepherd-king and giant-killer, assumed the mantle of teacher and began to train his troops.

David's passion in life was to live in the presence of the Lord, to provide a dwelling place for Jehovah in his heart and in Jerusalem. This seed was planted when he was a young shepherd boy, watered by Samuel's anointing, matured by Saul's pursuit and harvested with God's deliverance. David developed a heart attitude that moved God to action and produced blessings abundantly.

David was willing to place his faith in the King of Kings and pay whatever price was necessary.

At times the price was almost more than David could bear. He forgot his duties as commander in chief, lusted after and committed adultery with Bathsheba, wife of Uriah the Hittite—a loyal warrior—and then had placed him in position to be killed during the battle at Rabbah (II Samuel 11-12.) A holy God could not ignore the sins of His chosen king; David had to be chastised for his sins. The first blow was the death of the child conceived in adultery.

Nathan, the prophet, strode into the presence of the king and challenged David with a parable designed to provoke either hard-heartedness or repentance. The "man after God's own heart," chose the path of repentance, but was unable to escape the consequences of sin. God had given Nathan a message to deliver:

> "'Now, therefore, the sword will never depart from your
> house, because you despised me and took the wife of Uriah
> the Hittite to be your own.' This is what the LORD says: 'Out
> of your own household I am going to bring calamity upon

you. Before your very eyes I will take your wives and give them to one who is close to you, and he will lie with your wives in broad daylight,'" (2 Samuel 12:10-11, NIV).

David refused to make excuses for his behavior. He bowed his head in abject anguish and regret and whispered:

"I have sinned against the LORD," (II Samuel 12:13, NIV.)

The confrontation with Nathan elicited one of the most moving Psalms attributed to the king, Psalm 51:

Have mercy on me, O God, according to your unfailing love; according to your great compassion blot out my transgressions. Wash away all my iniquity and cleanse me from my sin. For I know my transgressions, and my sin is always before me. Against you, you only, have I sinned and done what is evil in your sight; so you are right in your verdict and justified when you judge.... Cleanse me with hyssop, and I will be clean; wash me, and I will be whiter than snow. Create in me a pure heart, O God, and renew a steadfast spirit within me. Do not cast me from your presence or take your Holy Spirit from me..... You do not delight in sacrifice, or I would bring it; you do not take pleasure in burnt offerings. My sacrifice, O God, is a broken spirit; a broken and contrite heart you, God, will not despise, (Psalm 51:1-4, 7, 10-11, 16-17.).

The sword would fall again when Amnon, David's son by Ahinoam, raped his half-sister Tamar, daughter of Maacah. David had coveted the beautiful Bathsheba; Amnon lusted after his sibling—and so began the fulfillment of Nathan's prophecy. Like his father before him, Amnon failed to control his desire. Perhaps as the result of a guilty conscience, David was incapable of meting out punishment to Amnon. His failure incensed his son Absalom, Tamar's brother who found the injustice intolerable.

And so fell another blow as predicted by Nathan. David had plotted the murder of Uriah to cover his sin; Absalom murdered Amnon in retaliation for his heinous and incestuous crime.

Anger drove Absalom to try to wrest the kingdom of Judah from his father. Filled with pride and egotism, driven by wrath, blinded by his own good looks, proud of his long, luxuriant mane of hair, besotted with power, Absalom decided he was above the law. Exiled to his mother's homeland of Geshur, he languished there for three years while nurturing a loathing for his father. When Absalom was allowed to return, his animosity was aggravated by rumors that God had chosen Solomon, his half-brother as David's successor. So strong was his abhorrence that he determined to unseat his father and then set a scheme in action to do so. Once he had accomplished his aim of driving David from Jerusalem and wresting the kingdom from him, Absalom was counseled to do something so odious that it should have ensured David's lifetime loathing—he was advised to openly lie with David's concubines who had been left behind to watch over the king's house.

When troops loyal to David gathered in battle against the army of Absalom, David waited anxiously for word of his son's safety. Like the father of the prodigal son, he longed for the return and repentance of his son; but unlike that father, David's desire was not to be granted. A messenger arrived from the battlefront to inform the exiled king that while fleeing the skirmish, Absalom's hair had become entangled in the branches of a tree. Held captive by his tresses, the presumptuous young man was hacked to death by his pursuers.

David was heartbroken and fell into deep and bitter mourning, and in his grief, he forgave:

> The king was overcome with emotion. He went up to the
> room over the gateway and burst into tears. And as he went,
> he cried, "O my son Absalom! My son, my son Absalom! If
> only I had died instead of you! O Absalom, my son, my son,"
> (II Samuel 18:33, NLT.)

In II Samuel 19, David was finally able to return to Jerusalem after Absalom's death. Betrayed by his son, banished from the throne, expelled from Jerusalem, still David mourned the loss of his son more than his kingship. The consequences of sin weighed heavily on his heart.

Near the end of his life, David desired to build a permanent home for God in Jerusalem—a Temple worthy of the King of the Universe, an edifice in appreciation for God's great blessings in his life. He shared this desire with the prophet Nathan. In a dream, God advised the prophet that David's successor, Solomon, would be the one to build the Temple. David was crushed. He could have gone off in a huff, angry with God for not honoring his request. Not David; he amassed a large quantity of precious metals—gold and silver—and precious stones with which to build and adorn the Temple. By today's standards, this totaled approximately three thousand tons of gold and thirty thousand tons of silver. He gathered and stockpiled other materials his son Solomon would need to erect the house of God:

> David gave orders to gather together the aliens who were residing in the land of Israel, and he set stonecutters to prepare dressed stones for building the house of God. David also provided great stores of iron for nails for the doors of the gates and for clamps, as well as bronze in quantities beyond weighing, and cedar logs without number — for the Sidonians and Tyrians brought great quantities of cedar to David (I Chronicles 22:2-4, NRSV.)

David didn't let disappointment stand in the way of gratitude for all the blessings Jehovah had bestowed upon him. Don't allow anything the Enemy may place in your pathway to rob you of a commanded blessing from a loving Father. Solomon wrote:

> If your enemy is hungry, give him bread to eat; and if he is thirsty, give him water to drink; for so you will heap coals of fire on his head, and the LORD will reward you (Proverbs 25:21-22, NKJV.)

David gave lavishly, although he did not live to see the fruits of his labor. The Temple was built and sumptuously furnished due to his sacrificial offering.

In the midst of unrelenting opposition, David was able to accomplish great things for his King, and he remained pliable in the hands of God and was rewarded with a commanded blessing.

CHAPTER 9

THE BLESSINGS
FROM PRAYER

The prayer of a righteous person is powerful and effective.

(JAMES 5:16B, NIV)

D aniel—just the name brings visions of young Hebrews forced into
service to a heathen king, fiery furnaces, handwriting on walls,
prophecies of future events, and hungry lions. It also speaks of faithfulness to Jehovah, of steadfastness in the face of persecution, and of a dedicated prayer life. The book of Daniel reveals the struggle between good
and evil, between the messenger of God and the messenger of Satan, and
of the triumph of righteousness.

The fiery dart that launched my own persecution and "lion's den" expe-
rience was flung by none other than Ruth Carter Stapleton, the late sister of
President Jimmy Carter. She and I had spoken at a rally in Giants Stadium in
New Jersey. She was there to encourage people to join her on a tour to Israel.
As a lead-in to that, Ruth said excitedly, "I am going to announce today that
I will visit Mike Evans' headquarters at Stoneybrook on Long Island to tell
Jews about Jesus."

Several Jewish organizations were upset about Ruth's announcement.
They lobbied the president to stop her by asking Prime Minister Menachem

Begin to call Mr. Carter and protest her participation in the Long Island event. It was truly like being in the midst of a den of hungry lions, and the night had not yet passed.

Before the trip to Long Island materialized, Ruth flew to New York City and strongly denounced me as a cult leader akin to Reverend Moon, the leader of the Moonies. She said I had deceived her, and summarily cancelled her appearance with me. Her publicist tried to bolster my shattered spirit. "It's politics, Mike! Don't take it personally." The next fourteen months were a living hell. I began to receive death threats. The Long Island Council of Churches turned against me. My denomination turned against me. Yet, each time God delivered me, each fiery trial that was overcome, each time He shut the mouths of the hungry lions, I was reminded through His Word of all the promises that are mine.

In Scripture, the lives of Daniel, Shadrach, Meshach, and Abednego reflect their commitment to prayer and to trust in Yahweh—from birth and captivity until death. Submission to Jehovah was far from easy. The dedicated young Hebrew men were ridiculed, bullied, and goaded to conform to Babylonian ways, but chose instead to remain faithful to the God of Abraham, Isaac, and Jacob. It was preferable to offering obeisance to the gods of the Babylonians. When we study the book of Daniel we see it as a treatise on the End Times; however, it is also an in-depth study on obedience.

Daniel and his three companions were among the scores carried off to Babylon by Nebuchadnezzar's armies. They were snatched from their homes and families; we are not told if their relatives survived the battle and ransacking of Jerusalem. These Hebrew boys from noble, nurturing families had been accustomed to a warm and caring atmosphere. They were homesick and unsettled, and things would only get worse. Their familial protection had been stripped from them, and they were at the mercy of a pagan king and his minions. Yet God had not forsaken them; their training had not abandoned them; their faith in Jehovah was secure. They would be faced with trials and demands that would challenge their beliefs—yet they would stand strong.

One of the first tests Daniel and his friends would be subjected to was over the food provided them. The king had ordered that they be fed from his table:

> Then the king ordered Ashpenaz, chief of his court officials,
> to bring into the king's service some of the Israelites from the
> royal family and the nobility—young men without any physi-
> cal defect, handsome, showing aptitude for every kind of learn-
> ing, well informed, quick to understand, and qualified to serve
> in the king's palace. He was to teach them the language and
> literature of the Babylonians. The king assigned them a daily
> amount of food and wine from the king's table. They were to
> be trained for three years, and after that they were to enter the
> king's service. Among those who were chosen were some from
> Judah: Daniel, Hananiah, Mishael and Azariah. The chief offi-
> cial gave them new names: to Daniel, the name Belteshazzar;
> to Hananiah, Shadrach; to Mishael, Meshach; and to Azariah,
> Abednego, (Daniel 1:3–7, NIV.)

Daniel, Shadrach, Meshach, and Abednego were determined not to eat
the food offered to idols and petitioned the Babylonian official to allow them
to consume only vegetables and water. With reluctance, the keeper agreed.
The resolve of the young men and their obedience to God's law won them the
respect of Nebuchadnezzar and the official. They had passed the first test with
flying colors, but another, more difficult test lurked around the corner. How
would they handle a life-threatening situation?

Nebuchadnezzar was not unlike many politicians today: He began to
believe his own public relations hype. As his ego grew, so did his desire to
erect a memorial statue in accordance with his wealth and power. The artisans
loosely based the design of the image on a dream that Nebuchadnezzar had
experienced, the meaning of which Daniel had interpreted. The king opened
the doors to his vast storehouses of treasure to provide the materials from
which the idol was to be made. It is entirely possible that some of the golden
vessels taken from the Temple in Jerusalem were included in those melted and
used to fashion the graven image.

The Chaldeans worshipped a number of heathen deities, but nothing as
brilliant and magnificent as the statue that rose up from the plain of Dura. It
was ninety feet tall and nine feet wide—probably with an appearance much

like an obelisk. Nebuchadnezzar was elated with the statue when it was completed and issued an edict to the people of Babylon: The image was to be dedicated as an object of worship, and all would display their consummate devotion by bowing down before the image:

> As soon as you hear the sound of the horn, flute, zither, lyre, harp, pipe and all kinds of music, you must fall down and worship the image of gold that King Nebuchadnezzar has set up. Whoever does not fall down and worship will immediately be thrown into a blazing furnace, (Daniel 3:5–6, NIV.)

Now, Daniel and his friends had cut their teeth on the laws of God, specifically the Ten Commandments. Moses had instructed the children of Israel in Deuteronomy 11:19 that the Word of Jehovah was to be taught to the children "when you sit in your house, when you walk by the way, when you lie down, and when you rise up." The tenets and precepts of God's law were ingrained in the minds and spirit of those young men.

The first and second commandments are very specific:

> "You shall have no other gods before me. You shall not make for yourself an image in the form of anything in heaven above or on the earth beneath or in the waters below. You shall not bow down to them or worship them, (Exodus 20:3–5a, NIV.)

The day appointed by Nebuchadnezzar arrived accompanied by great pomp and ceremony. Off to one side of the dais from which the king held court was a reminder of the punishment for disobedience: the ovens into which those who refused to bow would be thrown. On the plain surrounding the image, the people gathered awaiting the strains of the musical instruments that were to signal the moment to fall on their faces and worship the golden statue.

The Powers of Darkness danced in anticipation of the destruction of the trio of Hebrews in the king's court—the men who were likely to refuse the order to bow. Satan probably gleefully waited with sulfurous breath to see the defeat of God's chosen people. The king had decreed compliance with his edict; God declared a different scenario. When Nebuchadnezzar looked out over the prostrate participants, he saw three young men standing tall— Shadrach, Meshach, and Abednego. They had determined not to disgrace the God of heaven. Jehovah was their Lord and King—they would bow to no other, they would pray to no other, they would serve no other.

Their detractors—those jealous of the honors that had been bestowed on Daniel and his companions—could not wait to advise the king that three of his subjects had dared to flagrantly defy his order:

> "But there are some Jews whom you have set over the affairs of the province of Babylon—Shadrach, Meshach and Abednego—who pay no attention to you, Your Majesty. They neither serve your gods nor worship the image of gold you have set up," (Daniel 3:12, NIV.)

Nebuchadnezzar's anger boiled. How dare they not obey his commandment! He ordered the men brought to stand in his presence. He demanded, "Is it true? Did you not bow down before the golden image as I ordered? Do you not know the punishment that awaits you if you refuse to bow?"

Shadrach, Meshach, and Abednego quietly explained to the king that they could not bow to any image because of their fidelity to Jehovah God. Nebuchadnezzar's visage grew darker as he pointed toward the ovens burning brightly in the distance. He ordered the musicians to play again in order to give these three young men a second chance to adhere to his instructions. Again they refused. As they stood before the king, the three Hebrew men replied:

> "King Nebuchadnezzar, we do not need to defend ourselves before you in this matter. If we are thrown into the blazing furnace, the God we serve is able to deliver us from it, and He will deliver us from Your Majesty's hand. But even

if He does not, we want you to know, Your Majesty, that we
will not serve your gods or worship the image of gold you
have set up," (Daniel 3:16–18, NIV.)

Infuriated by their answer, the king ordered the ovens stoked seven
times hotter. He then commanded the mightiest men in his army to bind the
three men and toss them into the furnace. So hot was the fire that the men
who marched Shadrach, Meshach, and Abednego toward the flames were
killed. But God—(what a difference those two words can make)—But God
had not overlooked the fidelity of his children. As the men who stood strong
in His Name landed in the midst of the fire, He poured out His favor upon
them and joined them there. As the fire lapped up the bindings of His servants, Jehovah tamed the flames—they lost the ability to devour.

From his royal perch high above the furnace, the king watched in anticipation of seeing the three defiant Hebrews totally consumed by the raging
inferno. Suddenly, his triumph turned to fear. He grew pale as he lurched
from the throne and pointed toward the all-consuming flames. He stuttered,
"Did we not cast three men bound into the midst of the fire? ... Look!...I see
four men loose, walking in the midst of the fire; and they are not hurt, and
the form of the fourth is like the Son of God," (Daniel 3:24, 25, NKJV.)

Arthur Smith wrote a rousing spiritual about the experiences of the
Three Hebrew Children titled "The Fourth Man." The chorus reads:

They wouldn't bend. They held onto the will of God so
we are told. They wouldn't bow. They would not bow their
knees to the idol made of gold. They wouldn't burn. They
were protected by the fourth man in the fire. They wouldn't
bend, they wouldn't bow, they wouldn't burn.[16]

In utter amazement, the king abandoned his throne and strode across
the plain. He crept as close to the fire as he safely could and cried:

"Shadrach, Meshach and Abed-Nego, servants of the
Most High God, come out, and come here." Then Shadrach,

Meshach, and Abed-Nego came from the midst of the fire. And the satraps, administrators, governors, and the king's counselors gathered together, and they saw these men on whose bodies the fire had no power; the hair of their head was not singed nor were their garments affected, and the smell of fire was not on them, (Daniel 3:26–27, NKJV.)

Nebuchadnezzar was overwhelmed by the miracle that accompanied their deliverance by the Most High God. He decreed:

"Blessed be the God of Shadrach, Meshach, and Abed-Nego, who sent His Angel and delivered His servants who trusted in Him, and they have frustrated the king's word, and yielded their bodies, that they should not serve nor worship any god except their own God! Therefore I make a decree that any people, nation, or language which speaks anything amiss against the God of Shadrach, Meshach, and Abed-Nego shall be cut in pieces, and their houses shall be made an ash heap; because there is no other God who can deliver like this." Then the king promoted Shadrach, Meshach, and Abed-Nego in the province of Babylon, (Daniel 3:28–30, NKJV.)

Not yet done with the prayer warriors from Jerusalem, the Enemy would devise yet another test for Daniel just as life-threatening as the one faced by his friends. In Chapter 5 of Daniel, Babylon fell to the Medes and Persians. They took the entire kingdom without having launched an arrow or raised a lance. The prophet Isaiah cried, "Babylon is fallen, is fallen! And all the carved images of her gods He has broken to the ground," (Isaiah 21:9, NKJV.) Nebuchadnezzar's golden idols had been crushed into dust.

The amazing thing about the bloodless coup was how little it affected Daniel in the king's court. He survived the upheaval, and at the beginning of the chapter we read that he was appointed as one of three governors over the kingdom. The new king was Darius, who ruled contemporaneously with Cyrus.

One thing is clear throughout Daniel chapter 6: God rules! Nations rise and nations fall, but God's plan will go forward according to His timetable. That should give us great hope as we view Daniel exactly where God had placed him. We will also see that God is unfettered by Man's pronouncements. Darius, the new leader, was a man of power and organization; he had great skill and intellect. He held no loyalty to the God of Israel, and yet as we read in the sixth chapter, we find that he had knowledge of Daniel's Jehovah.

Daniel was no longer a young man. It is likely that he was nearing ninety years of age. Through all the intervening years, he had remained faithful to God and was a committed witness and dedicated prayer warrior. Far from being "on the shelf," his experience was utilized both by Darius and by God. We can see from his longevity in the Babylonian and then the Medo-Persian Empires that Daniel was a man of wisdom, a dynamic leader, and a capable administrator. Added to those traits was a close relationship to Jehovah, which afforded him the ability to interpret dreams and visions. He was God's man for that time and in that place. God turned the heart of Darius toward a Hebrew man and placed him in a strategic place of authority. The Bible reminds us in Proverbs 21:2 (NKJV), that the "king's heart is in the hand of the Lord...He turns it wherever He wishes."

Often when Believers are set in a place of authority, it is not long before the Enemy raises his ugly head, determined to target the faithful—and Daniel was no exception. Soon others in the court were plotting:

> So the governors and satraps sought to find some charge against Daniel concerning the kingdom; but they could find no charge or fault, because he was faithful; nor was there any error or fault found in him. Then these men said, "We shall not find any charge against this Daniel unless we find it against him concerning the law of his God," (Daniel 6:4–5, NKJV.)

There were no charges of adultery; no Watergate break-ins, no

Iran-Contra Affairs, no hidden bodies in the attic. The accusers could find
no fault in Daniel; his life was exemplary. He was a member in good standing
of the Fellowship of the Offenders—his dedication to Yahweh was certainly
offensive to the Babylonians. They had to resort to subterfuge in order to trap
their rival. Daniel was known abroad for his custom of praying with his face
toward Jerusalem three times each day. The pattern had been established. So
his adversaries took advantage of Daniel's routine and approached the king:

> "King Darius, live forever! All the governors of the king-
> dom, the administrators and satraps, the counselors and
> advisors, have consulted together to establish a royal statute
> and to make a firm decree, that whoever petitions any god
> or man for thirty days, except you, O king, shall be cast into
> the den of lions. Now, O king, establish the decree and sign
> the writing, so that it cannot be changed, according to the
> law of the Medes and Persians, which does not alter," (Dan-
> iel 6:6–8, NKJV.)

Sneaky, weren't they? And, of course, the king was flattered by all this
attention. Who wouldn't want to be God for a month! Obviously, Darius
wanted all the accolades and adoration, so he succumbed to the temptation
and signed the decree. He was swept away on a tide of ego and pressed his
signet ring into the wax on a document that would become law, one which
could not be changed. The thing was done—bow to any God except Darius
and become lion fodder.

When Daniel heard of the new law that had been imposed, what do you
suppose he did—wring his hands and cry, "Why me, God?" Did he begin to
look for a secret place to pray? No! Verse 10 says:

> Now when Daniel knew that the writing was signed, he
> went home. And in his upper room, with his windows open
> toward Jerusalem, he knelt down on his knees three times
> that day, and prayed and gave thanks before his God, as was
> his custom since early days, (Daniel 6:10, NKJV.)

Bible lecturer, Frank Wallace, wrote of Daniel:

> The secret of his power and of his faithfulness,...was his private life in prayer that was never hindered....It was not a sudden burst of energy in prayer because the circumstances were difficult and his life was in danger, it was his continual practice. It was not something that was forced upon him, it was his joy.....I am perfectly sure that Daniel allowed nothing to interfere with the moments when he bowed his knees in prayer before his God. He was a great man, he had great responsibilities in administration and yet he could find time, three times a day, in settled portions to pray. We do not know how long, but he did it, it was his settled life, praying, praying, praying.[17]

Fear did not reign in Daniel's life; he was no "secret servant." God had been faithful to him and to his friends, and he had no reason to doubt. Either he would be preserved in the lion's den, or he would not, but Daniel was committed to doing the will of God. He refused to compromise his beliefs to gain the favor of the king.

The obvious happened: The men who had lain in wait for Daniel to make a misstep were overjoyed. Daniel knelt in his window in open view of passersby, his face toward the Holy City according to I Kings 8:46-49 (NLT):

> But in that land of exile, they might turn to you in repentance and pray, 'We have sinned, done evil, and acted wickedly.' If they turn to you with their whole heart and soul in the land of their enemies and pray toward the land you gave to their ancestors—toward this city you have chosen, and toward this Temple I have built to honor your name—then hear their prayers and their petition from heaven where you live, and uphold their cause.

Seeing Daniel in earnest prayer, the instigators gleefully ran to the king:

"Have you not signed a decree that every man who petitions any god or man within thirty days, except you, O king,
shall be cast into the den of lions? ... That Daniel, who is one
of the captives from Judah, does not show due regard for you,
O king, or for the decree that you have signed, but makes his
petition three times a day," (Daniel 6:11, 13, NKJV.)

Does that statement smack of anti-Semitism, of hatred for the Hebrews
that were unwitting captives in the land? The combination of envy and
enmity produced exultation from those who had devised the plan. The
trap had been set; Daniel had fallen into it—enemy vanquished, or so they
thought.

Darius likely felt as though he had been hit right in the solar plexus! He
was stunned by this turn of events: A man he greatly admired was now in
dire straits because of Darius' egotism.

Daniel's detractors were shouting, "That Hebrew, that foreigner, refused
to obey the king! Now you must obey the decree you have signed and toss
him to the lions." Daniel was summarily arrested and led to the lair where
the lions were penned. He was cast inside and a stone was brought to seal
the mouth of the den. Let me assure you that these were not lion cubs, nor
were there only one or two in the den, as we often see in illustrations. There
were a sufficient number of lions to rip Daniel to shreds and devour him in
a matter of minutes.

King Darius then sealed it with his signet ring and returned to the palace. So distressed was the king that he spent the night silently fasting. In
other words, in his sleeplessness he didn't call for the musicians, or the
dancing girls, or other diversions. The Bible says, "And he could not sleep."
I can believe he spent the night pacing in his bedchamber. At the earliest
opportunity, he burst forth from his room and went in search of an answer:

At the first light of dawn, the king got up and hurried
to the lions' den. When he came near the den, he called to
Daniel in an anguished voice, "Daniel, servant of the living
God, has your God, whom you serve continually, been able

to rescue you from the lions?" Daniel answered, "May the king live forever! My God sent his angel and he shut the mouths of the lions. They have not hurt me, because I was found innocent in his sight. Nor have I ever done any wrong before you, Your Majesty," (Daniel 6:19–22, NIV.)

Doesn't it seem a bit late for Darius to question Daniel's survival? It seems that every seed Daniel had sown into the king's life erupted at the mouth of the lion's den in the words, "Daniel, servant of the living God, has your God, whom you serve…" He wanted to know if everything Daniel had said to him was true. Could the living God deliver, do the miraculous, save the endangered? Darius had his answer as soon as he heard the words, "My God sent His angel, and he shut the mouths of the lions."

There is no record that Daniel offered any argument to the king before he was led away to the lion's den; only after God had vindicated him and saved him from the jaws of the ferocious beasts did he offer any defense. He knew he had been innocent of anything other than obedience to Jehovah-Shammah, the Lord who was present in the lion's den. Daniel had sought the kingdom of God and had been rewarded. Daniel's persistence in prayer won the favor of the king, but more importantly, it brought a commanded blessing.

CHAPTER 10

RIGHTEOUSNESS BRINGS BLESSINGS

It was by faith that Abel brought a more acceptable offering to God than Cain did. Abel's offering gave evidence that he was a righteous man, and God showed his approval of his gifts. Although Abel is long dead, he still speaks to us by his example of faith.

(PSALM 23:3, ESV.)

s a soldier in the United States army, I spent fourteen months in South Korea on a mountain the Koreans called Wong Tong Nee. Early one morning as I wandered around the mountain, not even thinking about God or my encounter with Jesus as a child, I faced something I had not experienced since Jesus had visited me. It was the overwhelming presence of God settling over me, and the burning desire to be a man of righteousness and integrity. Joy unspeakable filled my soul, and like Samuel of old, my spirit whispered, "Speak, Lord, for thy servant heareth," (1 Samuel 3:10, KJV.) Finding a secluded spot, I sank to the ground and tears streamed down my face as Jesus gently reminded me of His words when He had appeared to me as a child.

I whispered, "Jesus, will you ever talk to me audibly again? I need to hear Your voice. I sense the same presence I did when I was eleven." He did not answer me clearly, but suddenly I felt impressed by the Holy Spirit to turn to Daniel 10:9. With tears misting my eyes, I read, "Yet I heard the sound of his words; and while I heard the sound of his words I was in a deep sleep on my face, with my face to the ground. Suddenly, a hand touched me, which made me tremble on my knees and on the palms of my hands. And he said to me, 'O Daniel, man greatly beloved, understand the words that I speak to you, and stand upright, for I have now been sent to you.'" While He was speaking this word to me, I stood trembling and weeping. Eventually, the sensation of God's presence lifted, but I was at peace.

I was eager to hear the voice of God again; it would give me the affirmation I desperately needed in order to overcome. And I desperately wanted to receive a commanded blessing in my life, such as the one I had read about in Psalm 133.

The Spirit of God I had just experienced on Wong Tong Nee was the same presence I had encountered in my bedroom—first the presence, then the voice. Now I had experienced His presence, but where was His voice? I wanted to walk uprightly before my God, and I craved His direction.

Before leaving the spot that day, I gathered twelve stones and set up a small altar. Sometime during the day, every day, I returned to that spot to pray and seek God.

God is sovereign, and it is He who determines the number of our days. Abel's life was merely a vapor, but the story of his righteousness is told often. One of the earliest examples the Scriptures gives us of a righteous man is Abel, the second son of Adam and Eve. In Hebrew, the name means "breath, or vapor," perhaps an indication of the shortness of his life. James wrote: "Your life is like the morning fog—it's here a little while, then it's gone," (James 4:14, NLT.)

Most of us are familiar with the first murder recorded in the Bible. Cain, the older brother, was a tiller of the ground—a farmer; Abel was a keeper of sheep. Genesis does not tell us exactly how the two brothers knew what was considered a proper sacrifice to the most Holy God, but clearly they did. Perhaps Jehovah had given them instructions when He offered a blood sacrifice for the sin of Adam and Eve in the Garden.

As soon as the first couple realized the significance of their choice to defy God, they recognized that they were naked. In an attempt to hide their sin, the two covered themselves with fig leaves. (Couldn't they find anything else?) It was their way of handling their nakedness—the do-it-yourself way. However, God had a different plan. He killed an innocent animal—Genesis doesn't say what the animal was—and with the skin made "coats of skins" and clothed them. The lives of innocent animals were taken in order to cover the sin of Adam and Eve. It is a perfect picture of the obedience of Christ who would give His life to cover the sins of the world and make it possible for man to stand righteous before God, the Father.

The story of God's grace to their parents must have been told over and over to the two sons, Cain and Abel. Both had brought their sacrifices to present to Him, but each brought a different offering. Genesis 4:3 says that "Cain brought the fruit of the ground." He approached the altar of sacrifice with whatever came to hand. Rather than bringing the best of his crops at the beginning of the harvest, his gift was one of convenience—of show, one given not in faith, but in haste, a last-minute effort. Though he gave lip service to Jehovah, he was not a godly man; instead, he was quick to anger, self-indulgent, and jealous. Cain's wrathful response when God rejected his spur-of-the-moment offering was indicative of his character:

> But he did not accept Cain and his gift. This made Cain very angry, and he looked dejected. "Why are you so angry?" the LORD asked Cain. "Why do you look so dejected?" (Genesis 4:5–6, NLT.)

Cain was angry that God dared reject his offering. So indignant was he that he stood boldly at the altar and argued with the Creator of the universe. His anger and terrible attitude could not mask his knowledge that the requirements had not been met—and he knew that God knew. Even before Christ offered grace to everyone through His death on the cross, God offered Cain a second chance:

> "You will be accepted if you do what is right. But if you

refuse to do what is right, then watch out! Sin is crouching
at the door, eager to control you. But you must subdue it and
be its master," (Genesis 4:7, NLT.)

Cain could have reviewed the requirements for an acceptable offering,
humbled himself before God, and returned with a proper sacrifice. Instead,
he chose to stomp away with Jehovah's warning ringing in his ears. Sin
became his master and he responded accordingly.

Abel—both Matthew 23:35 and the writer of Hebrews (11:4) refer to
him as "righteous"—had made preparation for his offering. He had chosen a
firstborn from the flock. His offering was not a skinny, lame, marred sheep;
it was the best he had to offer. Abel approached the altar humbly and peni-
tently, bowed low in the presence of Almighty God, and presented his gift in
faith that his obedience would be honored—his gift accepted. God searched
the heart of Abel and saw righteousness, submission, and generosity. Abel
had presented a tithe of the very best of his livestock.

Abel's offering of a sheep was his way of acknowledging what God had
done in the Garden when He wrapped Adam and Eve in animal skins. He
presented an animal from his flock in both a thank offering and a sin offering. In essence, he was saying, "I want to be obedient. I am thanking You for
showing grace to my parents, and I am asking You to show the same grace
to me."

The two brothers walked away from the altar with totally different
countenances. Abel's was radiant with God's love and approval; Cain's was
dark, his face infused with rage, his heart filled with jealousy.

Solomon, the wise king, defined the effects of jealousy:

> Jealousy is cruel as the grave. Its flashes are flashes of
> fire, (Song of Solomon 8:6, RSV.)

Charles Swindoll wrote of jealousy:

> Jealousy and envy are often used interchangeably,
> but there is a difference. Envy begins with empty hands,

mourning for what it doesn't have. Jealousy is not quite the same. It begins with full hands but is threatened by the loss of its plenty. It is the pain of losing what I have to someone else, in spite of all my efforts to keep it....This was Cain's sin. He was jealous of Abel. He resented God's acceptance of his brother. No doubt his face was red with emotion and his eyes filled with rage as God smiled on Abel's sacrifice. Not until Abel's warm blood poured over Cain's cruel hands did jealousy subside.[18]

Abel's hands were raised in praise to Jehovah; Cain's fists were clenched in fury. He was so filled with resentment that he lured Abel into the field and murdered him.

Suddenly God called to Cain, "Where is Abel, your brother?"

A sullen Cain replied, "I don't have any idea. Why are you asking me, anyway? Am I my brother's keeper?" (Genesis 4:9, paraphrased.)

The punishment for Cain's crime was swift and severe. God stripped him of the land that he had tilled and banished him from His presence. He was consigned to be a vagrant and wanderer. And God warned:

"Therefore, whoever kills Cain, vengeance shall be taken on him sevenfold." And the LORD set a mark on Cain, lest anyone finding him should kill him, (Genesis 4:15, NKJV.)

When the horror of Cain's sin gripped him, he cried, "My punishment is greater than I can bear!" (Genesis 4:13, NKJV.)

Of the lives of Cain and Abel, noted Christian minister and author John MacArthur wrote:

Abel's sacrifice was accepted because he knew what God wanted and obeyed. Cain's was rejected because he knew what God wanted, yet disobeyed. To obey is righteous; to disobey is evil. Abel was of God; Cain was of Satan (1 John 3:12)... Abel offered a better sacrifice because it represented the obedience of faith. He willingly brought God what He asked, and he brought the very best that he had. In Abel's sacrifice, the way of the cross was first [foreshadowed.] The first sacrifice was Abel's lamb—one lamb for one person. Later came the Passover—with one lamb for one family. Then came the Day of Atonement—with one lamb for one nation. Finally came Good Friday—one Lamb for the whole world.[19]

If you wish to partake of the commanded blessings of a holy God and be commended as righteous, as was Abel, Proverbs 3:9-10 (NKJV) offers us a vitally important principle:

> Honor the LORD with your possessions, And with the firstfruits of all your increase; So your barns will be filled with plenty, And your vats will overflow with new wine.

His righteous response to God's command cost Abel's life but won him a place in the Bible's Hall of Heroes:

> By faith Abel brought God a better offering than Cain did. By faith he was commended as righteous, when God spoke well of his offerings. And by faith Abel still speaks, even though he is dead, (Hebrews 11:4, NIV.)

Abel responded to the call of God. His decision to obey regardless of the circumstances or the outcome led to his death, but it also produced great faith and an even greater reward.

David wrote often in Psalms of the abundant blessings accorded the righteous:

> Oh, continue your steadfast love to those who know you, and your righteousness to the upright of heart! (Psalm 36:10, ESV.)

The eyes of the LORD are on the righteous, and his ears
are attentive to their cry; 16 but the face of the LORD is
against those who do evil, to blot out their name from the
earth. 17 The righteous cry out, and the LORD hears them;
he delivers them from all their troubles. 18 The LORD
is close to the brokenhearted and saves those who are
crushed in spirit. 19 The righteous person may have many
troubles, but the LORD delivers him from them all; 20 he
protects all his bones, not one of them will be broken. 21
Evil will slay the wicked; the foes of the righteous will
be condemned. 22 The LORD will rescue his servants; no
one who takes refuge in him will be condemned, (Psalm
34:15-22, NIV.)

Better the little that the righteous have than the
wealth of many wicked; 17 for the power of the wicked
will be broken, but the LORD upholds the righteous. 18
The blameless spend their days under the LORD's care, and
their inheritance will endure forever. 19 In times of disaster they will not wither; in days of famine they will enjoy
plenty, (Psalm 37:16-19, NIV.)

Cast your burden on the LORD, And He shall sustain you;
He shall never permit the righteous to be moved, (Psalm
55:22.)

These are but a sampling of the verses, but it is sufficient to reveal
the commanded blessings enjoyed by the righteous, those who are in right
standing with God and who walk according to His precepts.

The wonderful attribute of God is that He is the one who determines
righteousness—not our family, not our friends, not our enemies, but God.
If we, as children of God desire a right relationship with Him, He is not
only willing, but eager, to reach out to us. Oh, the blessings of grace! While
we may question the efficacy of having some of the men and women God

declared righteous in the Scriptures—Rahab, Abraham, even Lot—these less-than-perfect individuals reached out to God and were rewarded when He graciously extended His hand to them. Each time one might have failed to meet the desired standard, God reached out again and again and extended mercy, and each time the wayward one returned to the fold. This, God reckoned as righteousness. He will do the same for you and me, if we are willing to get up and reach up. He will pour out a commanded blessing upon your life.

CHAPTER 11

GENEROSITY BRINGS BLESSINGS

So let each one give as he purposes in his heart, not grudgingly or of
necessity; for God loves a cheerful giver.

(II CORINTHIANS 9:7, NKJV)

The first war recorded in the Bible is found in Genesis chapter 14. Chedorlaomer, the king of Elam, had joined forces with five other kings in the region. They attacked the kings of Sodom and Gomorrah and after having put them to flight, sacked the cities and carried off the inhabitants. Among the captives were Abraham's nephew, Lot, and his family. Abraham might well have decided that Lot had made his own bed, and would therefore have to lie in it. After all, Lot had chosen to live in the city known for its deviant residents. He might have decided that he and his followers could never compete against such a vast army. Abraham did neither; instead, he summoned 318 of his trained servants and set out to rescue his family members.

When Jesus related the parable of the house built on the rock and the one built on the sand, He may well have been thinking of Abraham and his nephew. Lot had chosen to build his house on shaky ground, leaving himself vulnerable to thieves and looters. Abraham had built his house on the foundation rock of belief and faith in Jehovah, and was ready for the challenges ahead. He and his men pursued the marauders and rescued Lot, his family, and his possessions, as well as the king of Sodom and his subjects.

As Abraham was returning home, he was met by Melchizedek, who some say was Noah's son Shem. Others believe he was the pre-incarnate Christ. Whether he was God or simply a high priest, it is apparent that he was truly representative of a heavenly visitation with Abraham. The tired leader needed to be strengthened, comforted, and inspired. Often when you, child of God, have been wearied by the battle, strength comes through His Word or the tender ministrations of a servant of God.

We know with certainty that Melchizedek was at the very least a foreshadow of our Lord, as that is made apparent in Hebrews 7:1-3, NIV:

> This Melchizedek was king of Salem and priest of God Most High. He met Abraham returning from the defeat of the kings and blessed him, and Abraham gave him a tenth of everything. First, the name Melchizedek means "king of righteousness"; then also, "king of Salem" means "king of peace." Without father or mother, without genealogy, without beginning of days or end of life, resembling the Son of God, he remains a priest forever.

Abraham, like Melchizedek, was also a type of Christ. He pursued Lot, rescuing him from a life of bondage. Lot could not free himself; he was held captive by an evil king. Jesus Christ pursued you, who were dead in your trespasses and sin—bond slaves to Satan—and rescued you, not with troops and arms, but by His precious blood and through His unmerited grace. You were set free through the shedding of His blood and restored to the Kingdom of God.

As noted, the writer of Hebrews has described Melchizedek as having no father or mother. He seemed to have come from out of nowhere, for his genealogy is unknown. Secondly, he was said to be a priest of the Most High God and yet he was born before either Aaron or Levi. He asked Abraham for nothing. The Scriptures declare that it was Melchizedek who offered bread and wine—symbols of Christ's perfect sacrifice and obedience—to the weary warrior.

The King of Sodom had offered to reward Abraham with all the wealth that had been retrieved from the marauders. Abraham declined the offer made by the wicked ruler—with one exception: from that bounty, he took enough to feed his hungry troops and a portion to reward them for their labors. Humbled by the presence of the unassuming king of Salem, Abraham was constrained to offer one-tenth of all his personal wealth. The patriarch willingly presented the priest with a tithe some 430 years before the Mosaic Law commanded the practice. It was a willing gift to one who in Hebrews 5 is likened to Christ. How much more a holy privilege is it to present our tithes and offerings to our eternal High Priest! It is an act that calls forth the blessings of God.

Abraham chose to break bread with the King of Righteousness, Melchizedek, and honor him with an offering. He allied himself with the one who worshipped El Elyon, God Most High—the one who followed after the Supreme Ruler of the Universe. Along with the bread and wine, he offered a blessing:

"Blessed be Abram by God Most High, Creator of heaven
and earth. And praise be to God Most High, who delivered
your enemies into your hand," (Genesis 14:19–20, NIV.)

Abraham was rewarded with the commanded blessings of God. He gave from the abundance of his gratitude. Abraham knew that all he possessed was by the hand of Yahweh. He gave not because it was a law or commandment; he gave voluntarily and with confidence in God's abundant supply. It was an act of obedience and trust. The Creator responds to your gifts freely given. He welcomes your deliberate act of worship and consecration to Him. He blesses your generosity by bestowing His grace and favor on you.

God blesses us extravagantly. Not only did He give us the greatest gift Heaven could afford—our Lord—He also blessed those in the Bible who trusted Him. Our giving in return is an act of love and obedience and faith in God, virtues that the prince of this world does not have.

Before war, kings presented sacrifices (offerings), the acceptance of
which determined their success. David was no exception. He needed to
know that God would remember his offering. He needed victory in the battle. David felt unworthy, but he knew his feelings were not the determining
factor for victory—it was God's presence.

God challenges us to prove Him. What a statement—as if God needs to
prove anything. He instructed the Children of Israel:

> "Bring the whole tithe into the storehouse, that there
> may be food in my house. Test me in this, says the LORD
> Almighty, and see if I will not throw open the floodgates of
> heaven and pour out so much blessing that you will not have
> room enough for it," (Malachi 3:10, NIV.)

David prayed that Jehovah would remember our offerings. He knew an
offering that really challenges our faith is sacrificial. It is an inconvenient
offering, a faith offering, because we have to step out in faith to give it.
Sometimes that offering requires us to put our flesh on the altar.

A burnt offering was the Old Testament basis for hearing from Jehovah.
Our Lord's offering—that of a spotless, sacrificial Lamb—became the basis
of answered prayer for the world. We, then, are admonished to present our
bodies as an offering to God. Paul wrote:

> "I beseech you therefore, brethren, by the mercies of God,
> that you present your bodies a living sacrifice, holy, accept-
> able to God, which is your reasonable service," (Romans
> 12:1, NKJV.)

What a generous gift—yourself! When you think of what He has done
for you, is this too much to ask?

When we make Jesus Lord of everything—our life, finances, home, family—it is only then that we can say we are truly generous givers. It is then
that we are blessed by God:

"All these blessings will come on you and accompany you if you obey the Lord your God: You will be blessed in the city and blessed in the country. The fruit of your womb will be blessed, and the crops of your land and the young of your livestock—the calves of your herds and the lambs of your flocks. Your basket and your kneading trough will be blessed. You will be blessed when you come in and blessed when you go out. The Lord will grant that the enemies who rise up against you will be defeated before you. They will come at you from one direction but flee from you in seven. The Lord will send a blessing on your barns and on everything you put your hand to. The Lord your God will bless you in the land he is giving you," (Deuteronomy 28:2-8, NIV.)

As I have often said, "You can't out-give God." I can testify to the truth of that statement. Too often it is thought to be just monetary giving, but that is not the case. First and foremost, God wants the gift of *you*—your time, your knowledge, your gifts, your expertise. The most generous contributors have given their lives for the cause of the Gospel; others serve on mission fields at home and abroad. Many have given their time and talents to the Lord—preaching, singing, encouraging, ministering to the homeless, spending time daily in prayer and intercession.

Ten of Jesus' disciples gave their lives as martyrs to spread the Good News of His birth, death, and resurrection. Of the other two, Judas took his own life, and John died on the Isle of Patmos after having been beaten and abused for his faith. There is no greater gift than that of making the ultimate sacrifice. Unfortunately, as fanatic Islam spreads around the world today, rights of Christians have declined exponentially, and more are giving their lives. A 2010 ABC news story details how the Christian faith is taking a backseat to fanatical Islam:

In many countries through the Muslim world, religion has gained influence over governmental policy in the last

two decades. The militant Islamist group Hamas controls the Gaza Strip, while Islamist militias are fighting
the governments of Nigeria and the Philippines. Somalia,
Afghanistan, Pakistan and Yemen have fallen to a large
extent into the hands of Islamists. And where Islamists
are not yet in power, secular governing parties are trying to outstrip the more religious groups in a rush to the
Right.

This can be seen in Egypt, Algeria, Sudan, Indonesia, to
some extent, and also Malaysia. Even though this Islamiza-
tion often has more to do with politics than with religion,
and even though it doesn't necessarily lead to the persecution of Christians, it can still be said that where Islam gains
importance, freedoms for members of other faiths shrink.[20]

To the world, such generosity to the Church is senseless: "What? Give
abundant offerings? How are you going to pay your bills?" Let me encourage
you today. Giving opens the windows of heaven and brings God's blessings.
They may not just be monetary blessings... bargains come your way, unexpected gifts, or perhaps a better job.

The entire New Testament is filled with instances of unselfish giving:

> For God so loved the world that He *gave* His only begot-
> ten Son, that whoever believes in Him should not perish but
> have everlasting life (John 3:16, NKJV).

> Follow God's example, therefore, as dearly loved children
> and walk in the way of love, just as Christ loved us and *gave*
> himself up for us as a fragrant offering and sacrifice to God
> (Ephesians 5:1–2, NIV).

> I have shown you in every way, by laboring like this, that
> you must support the weak. And remember the words of the

LORD Jesus, that He said, "It is more blessed to *give* than to receive" (Acts 20:35, NKJV).

The Bible records God's promises concerning giving. It is not mere coincidence that the word *give* is found 880 times within its pages. The farmer sows extravagantly so that he can harvest abundantly. When he deposits one seed into the ground, he expects a plentiful return. When you practice sowing generously, you reap the rich, unmerited blessings of God. When you return to God a portion of your material blessings, you will recognize that "it is he who gives you the ability to produce wealth, and so confirms his covenant," (Deuteronomy 8:18, NIV.)

As Abraham received a blessing from Melchizedek, so those who give know how to receive from God. The spirit of giving releases a flood of blessing and you can, in turn, give of your time and your abilities. You can actually alter the effects of adversity and receive a commanded blessing by releasing a spirit of giving in every area of your life.

This ministry has been blessed with generous partners who have a deep, abiding love for Israel and her people. I had the privilege in late 2012 to join more than one hundred members in Jerusalem as we met with a number of Holocaust survivors. It is staggering to realize that there are more than 200,000 Holocaust survivors alive in Israel today. They are aged and frail, and most have no immediate family members still living—these are the survivors of Adolf Hitler's satanic attempt to destroy the Jewish people. When you meet these precious people and hug them, you can see the Nazi concentration camp identification numbers that were tattooed on their arms when they were young.

We gathered in a beautiful community center that will double as a bomb shelter when necessary. It was made available to them by loving friends, Jerusalem Prayer Team Partners. It was the first outreach project handled through the Jerusalem World Center, another JPT ministry project. The shelter has air-conditioning, heat, a kitchen, television, Internet, an air filtration system, beautiful bathrooms, and much more.

Earlier in the day, our group had visited Yad Vashem—the Holocaust Memorial in Jerusalem—a sobering reminder of man's inhumanity to God's chosen people. As we ministered to and prayed for these precious ones who had suffered so much, many eyes filled with tears. We were seeing before us people for whom those horrible days were not just stories but memories. Still, war has continued to threaten the Jewish people as tyrants and fanatics threaten to "wipe Israel off the map."

Not only has God blessed our Jerusalem Prayer Team partners, he has blessed this ministry with their wonderful spirit of giving, and their deep commitment to the Jewish people and to Israel.

CHAPTER 12

COURAGE BRINGS
BLESSINGS

"Arise, for this matter is your responsibility. We also are with you.
Be of good courage, and do it."

(EZRA 10:4)

The story of Esther is comparable to a modern fairy tale: A beautiful young Jewish girl is torn from her homeland and taken captive to Persia. A tyrannical ruler has banished his queen from her royal position and initiated a search for her successor. And of course, there is an evil villain, Haman, who desired to annihilate his enemies, the Jews.

The wealthy ruler of Persia, Ahasuerus (also known as Xerxes) decided in a fleeting moment of generosity to share his great treasure with his subjects. After seven days of gluttony and drunken revelry, the king commanded his beautiful queen, Vashti, to appear before the party goers. He wanted all of his beautiful treasures on display—including his stunning wife. She refused the king's request and was immediately banished from Ahasuerus' presence. The king was apparently crushed to lose his lovely queen but felt he had no choice in the matter: Her disobedience could not be tolerated. It would be seen as a weakness in the king's leadership ability.

The royal advisors decided Ahasuerus needed a diversion, a little something to take his mind off Vashti, and suggested a kingdom-wide search for a replacement. Upon his instruction a decree was issued:

> "Let beautiful young virgins be sought for the king,"
> (Esther 2:2, NKJV.)

Enter Esther, whose Hebrew name was Hadassah, which is derived from the word for "myrtle." She was aptly named, for the myrtle tree has leaves whose fragrance is only released when they are crushed. Esther was a Hebrew orphan who lived with her Uncle Mordecai. She and her people had been in captivity for over one hundred years when she was rounded up against her will, carried off to the palace in Shushan and placed in the house of the women under the care of the eunuch, Hegai. Esther could have wailed and pouted and bemoaned her fate, but instead, she retained a quiet, gentle and humble spirit. Hegai was so captivated by the lovely young woman that he took exceptional care of her, even going so far as giving her a special place in the harem. It was from there that, after twelve months of intensive beauty treatments, Esther was selected to spend a night with the king. When she was summoned to the royal bedchamber, Hegai took care to advise her on how to win Ahasuerus' attention. She was obedient to Hegai's suggestions and so captured the king's notice that she gained favor and was chosen as queen to replace Vashti.

Esther and Ahasuerus were not the only characters necessary to the plot; now we are introduced to Haman. He was the highest official in the kingdom—the personification of pride and lust for power. When Esther's uncle had refused to bow down to Haman, the egotistical official determined that the entire Jewish race would suffer his vengeance. What he didn't know was that the king owed Mordecai a great debt of gratitude for having once saved his life, a debt that had not been repaid. Mordecai had overheard a plot to kill the king and duly reported it. His actions were recorded in the chronicles of the king; little did he know they would eventually bring blessings to him and to his people.

Haman was unaware of Mordecai's deed; he knew only that the Jew failed to bow in his presence. Thus began the plot to destroy an entire people:

Then Haman said to King [Ahasuerus], "There is a certain people dispersed and scattered among the peoples in
all the provinces of your kingdom whose customs are different from those of all other people and who do not obey
the king's laws; it is not in the king's best interest to tolerate
them," (Esther 3:8, NIV1984.)

The king, unaware of Haman's true intent, agreed to the plan and issued
a proclamation to that effect. The news of the scheme soon reached Mordecai,
who carried the information to his niece.

Esther's uncle challenged the queen to approach Ahasuerus (a move
that could be punishable by death) and ask for the salvation of her people.
In encouraging her to do so, Mordecai confronted Esther with these timeless
words:

"For if you remain silent at this time, relief and deliverance for the Jews will arise from another place, but you and
your father's family will perish. And who knows but that you
have come to your royal position for such a time as this?"
(Esther 4:14, NIV.)

Esther reminded Mordecai that to approach the king without being summoned could cost the queen her life. She had not yet revealed to Ahasuerus
that she was a Jewess; that knowledge could also have meant instant death,
and yet she chose to obey her uncle. She was willing to sacrifice herself
to save her people. Her only request was that the Jews gather together to
fast and pray with her and her handmaidens. Her response to Mordecai was
magnificent:

"Go, gather together all the Jews who are in Susa, and
fast for me. Do not eat or drink for three days, night or day.
I and my attendants will fast as you do. When this is done, I
will go to the king, even though it is against the law. And if
I perish, I perish," (Esther 4:16, NIV.)

On the third day, Esther dressed in her most beautiful gown, wrapped herself with royal robes, and then with confidence stepped into the throne room. Seeing his beautiful queen slip into the hall pleased Ahasuerus and he extended his golden scepter in her direction. She stepped forward with assurance and touched the staff to obtain the pardon it offered her. The king asked, "What do you desire? I will give you up to half my kingdom."

Rather than respond directly to Ahasuerus' offer, Esther instead invited him and Haman to join her in her quarters for a banquet. When the day arrived, the king again offered Esther up to half his kingdom. Again she requested their presence at a second banquet, and then informed the king that she would make her request known to him.

Ahasuerus must have been a bit baffled, but so engaging was Esther that he complied. Haman's ego was so inflated at having been given special attention by the queen that he set off for home in a cloud of self-aggrandizement. As he left the palace, he saw Mordecai sitting at the gate. Haman's entire evening must have been ruined when once again, the Jew failed to bow down at his passing. He was enraged because he had not received the honor he thought due him.

While Haman pouted and plotted against the Jews, the king discovered that Mordecai had never been rewarded for having saved his life. To determine how best to honor Mordecai, Ahasuerus asked Haman:

> "What shall be done for the man whom the king delights
> to honor?" (Esther 6:6, NKJV.)

The Bible records that the self-centered Haman said to himself:

> "Whom would the king delight to honor more than me?"
> (Esther 6:6, NKJV.)

Certain that he would be granted all the things on his personal bucket list—fame, power, and wealth—Haman continued:

> "If the king wishes to honor someone, he should bring

out one of the king's own royal robes, as well as a horse that the king himself has ridden—one with a royal emblem on its head. Let the robes and the horse be handed over to one of the king's most noble officials. And let him see that the man whom the king wishes to honor is dressed in the king's robes and led through the city square on the king's horse. Have the official shout as they go, 'This is what the king does for someone he wishes to honor!'" (Esther 6:7–9, NLT.)

With chest puffed out, Haman waited for the king to announce that he was the one to be acclaimed. Imagine his fury when Ahasuerus calmly announced that the man to be honored was none other than Mordecai. Delighted with Haman's answer, the king shouted:

"Quick! Take the robes and my horse, and do just as you have said for Mordecai the Jew, who sits at the gate of the palace. Leave out nothing you have suggested!" (Esther 6:10, NLT.)

Haman was humiliated! After doing the king's bidding, he crept off home to his family and friends for a big pity party. They did not have long to console him, for soon after his arrival the queen's footmen would arrive to carry him to the second banquet.

As Esther wined and dined her guests, the king asked the nature of her request and again offered her up to half of his kingdom. This time she did not hesitate:

"If I have found favor with you, Your Majesty, and if it pleases you, grant me my life—this is my petition. And spare my people—this is my request. For I and my people have been sold to be destroyed, killed and annihilated. If we had merely been sold as male and female slaves, I would have kept quiet, because no such distress would justify disturbing the king," (Esther 7:3–4, NIV.)

Ahasuerus was stunned! Who would dare threaten the queen? Esther promptly pointed a finger at the culprit and confirmed it was:

> "An adversary and enemy! This vile
> Haman!" (Esther 7:6, NIV.)

> The king was enraged. He rose from the banquet table and stalked out into the palace garden. Haman, in fear for his life, threw himself on the couch on which Esther reclined and began to plead with her. At that moment the king returned to the hall, and seeing Haman on the couch screamed, "Will he even molest the queen while she is with me in the house?" (Esther 7:8b, NIV.)

Now, Haman had ordered a long pole about 75 feet high erected near his house for the express purpose of impaling Mordecai. One of the queen's eunuchs informed the king of the pole and its purpose. Ahasuerus immediately ordered that Haman be impaled on the pole meant for Mordecai. The grisly sentence was carried out forthwith.

Esther had then turned to the king and informed him of Haman's evil plot to destroy the Jews, her people. Unfortunately, the king could not rescind the original decree, but he issued a second set of orders that permitted the Jews to fight for their lives against their enemies. The Jews armed themselves and routed the opposition on the 13th of Adar. On the 14th of Adar, a fete was held to celebrate their victory. A royal celebration was also held in Susa; Mordecai was honored by the king; and Esther was given all of Haman's properties and wealth.

If we could, we might ask Esther if courage brought the blessings of God. She came to the king in mortal fear, yet determined to save her kinsmen, and she left with supernatural favor. She came in despair and left rejoicing. She came representing a people who were marked for destruction and left the king's presence with a pardon.

Esther obeyed at the risk of her own life so that the Jews might be spared the edge of the sword. She had learned that inner peace was not the absence of conflict; it was having the courage to face the problem and make the right choices. Esther's courage brought the blessings of God, not only into her life, but the lives of her people, the Jews. Still today, the feast of Purim is celebrated in honor of the deliverance of the Jews in Persia. Traditionally, Jews commemorate Purim with the reading of the Book of Esther, giving gifts of food, candy, and pastries, and sharing with the poor.

Under the tutelage of Mordecai and then Hegai, Esther accepted instruction with a spirit that was godly and teachable. She exhibited amazing strength and courage. Her humility was so striking that she easily won the respect of others, and ultimately became queen. With Haman's wicked plot and evil plans, we see why God chose this beautiful, courageous woman as His instrument. It was these attributes—obedience, humility, courage and determination—that saved her people from destruction and won the blessings of God. Esther had indeed, come to the kingdom for just such a time.

My own "for such a time as this" moment occurred in 1981, when my ministry had been threatened with disaster because of lies. I was more in need than ever of God's blessings in my life. After much prayer and then being prodded by the Spirit of God to request a meeting with Prime Minister Menachem Begin, I flew to New York en route to Israel and took a room at the Plaza Hotel to pray. The following morning as I sat in the hotel, reading my Bible, God again gave me the same scripture He had given me in the past:

> But those who wait on the Lord shall renew their strength;
> they shall mount up with wings like eagles, they shall run
> and not be weary, they shall walk and not faint (Isaiah 40:31,
> NKJV.)

I sent a wire to the prime minister's office requesting a meeting and advising him of where I would be staying. I didn't know if he would see me, but I was going to do what God had directed me to do.

Now, I had never met Menachem Begin and had no idea why he would ever want to meet with me, an unknown Christian minister. I wasn't a Rev. Billy Graham or a noted politician—just a guy from the other side of the tracks determined to obey the call of God.

Several days later, I set off for the airport and the encounter that would provide the focus of my life and ministry. After a long and tiring flight, I checked in to a hotel in Jerusalem and began to pray. For a week I prayed and fasted in my hotel room.

One morning the phone rang shrilly. A voice on the other end said, "Mike Evans? This is Yehiel Kadashai, Prime Minister Begin's personal secretary. The prime minister has agreed to meet with you. Are you available this afternoon?"

My heart stood still. I stammered, "Yes, what time should I come?"

Mr. Kadashai confirmed a time, and I dropped the handset back in the cradle. My knees turned to jelly and I sank down on the bed. I was going to meet the prime minister of Israel! God had honored His promise to me. It was the beginning of a friendship that lasted until Mr. Begin's death, and it opened door after door for me in the nation of Israel. God's blessings are most often apparent when we are in a place of brokenness, as was Esther, and as was I. It is then that the hand of God reaches out to us in grace to lift us up.

CHAPTER 13

BLESSED WITH
REUNIFICATION &
RESTORATION

"Like birds flying about, So will the LORD of hosts defend Jerusalem.
Defending, He will also deliver it; Passing over, He will preserve it."

(ISAIAH 31:5, NKJV)

Since the British partition of Palestine in 1947, the city of Jerusalem had been divided. Jerusalem had a knife thrust through her heart. Jews were not allowed near the Western Wall to pray and conditions in the Jordanian-controlled portion of the city were abysmal. It would remain that way until reunified during the 1967 Six Day War when God blessed His people with a victory that would restore the Holy City.

In mid-April 1967 Soviet Ambassador to Israel Leonid Chuvakhin complained to Prime Minister Levi Eshkol about a purported buildup of arms and troops on the Syrian border. Eshkol offered to drive him to the Syrian border to show him that the accusations were untrue. Apparently Ambassador Chuvakhin had no need to learn the truth; the abounding rumors were enough to satisfy him. It was, however, a useful diplomatic tool: If the rumors of Israeli aggression failed to materialize, the Soviets could brag that it was their support of the Syrian Ba'athist regime that saved the day.

The Soviets, however, heated the kettle just a tad too long and it boiled over and scalded them. Egyptian President Gamal Abdul Nasser amassed an army on the Sinai Peninsula, opposite Israel's border. He closed the Strait at Sharm El-Sheikh at the mouth of the Gulf of Aqaba. His moves were classic provocations. Israel had already notified the UN Security Council that if measures warranted, it would act in its own self-defense. UN Secretary General U Thant failed to act forcefully to execute the conditions of a truce that had existed since 1956. The UN peacekeeping forces standing between Nasser's army and the Israelis timidly packed up their tents and left town. On May 19, 1967, nothing stood between the Egyptians and the border of Israel.

In an amazing display of self-assurance, Prime Minister Levi Eshkol and Defense Minister Moshe Dayan remained cool, not acting until every alternative to avoid a confrontation had proved fruitless. On May 30 King Hussein of Jordan, at first reluctant to join the Arab coalition, flew to Cairo to mend fences with Nasser and sign a mutual defense pact. Israeli intelligence, headed by Isser Harel, had spent a considerable amount of time studying the Arab character. They knew, for instance, that collective efforts among Arabs were seldom cohesive for any length of time. The best the Israelis could hope for was that the pact would be Hussein's lone demonstration of Arab solidarity—and he would leave the fighting to Egypt and Syria.

Israel launched a lightning attack against the Arab states at 7:10 on the morning of June 5th. Well before noon nearly the entire Egyptian aircraft fleet was a flaming wreckage. Its air force had been destroyed on the ground by Israeli fighter jets, as God blinded the eyes of the Egyptians to the coming assault. In similar attacks, Israel destroyed Syrian jets and Jordanian planes.

Simultaneously, Israeli ground forces struck the Egyptian army amassed in the Sinai with a fist that virtually demolished Egypt's capacity to respond. As an important part of Israeli strategy for victory, Dayan had ordered a complete blackout of news. None of the stunning victories of June 5 were acknowledged for a twenty-four hour period. They allowed to go unchallenged loudly-proclaimed Egyptian announcements boasting it had destroyed Israel's armed forces. The Israelis wanted to forestall a Soviet move toward a cease-fire, and let it think its client states were winning the war.

Dayan's ploy had one unexpected drawback: King Hussein had also heard Radio Cairo's bizarre and whimsical interpretation of the facts and believed the reports. Israel had already contacted the king and offered not to infringe on his territory if he would stay put. Perhaps out of a desire for self-glory, Hussein ignored Israel's proposal and instructed his troops to begin shelling West Jerusalem. Hoping that was the limit of Hussein's military action, Dayan ordered the front commander in Jerusalem, Uzi Narkiss, to hold his fire. But just to be on the safe side, Israeli jets destroyed Amman's air force of twenty Hunter jets the same day.

At one o'clock that afternoon, the Jordanians made their move to over-run Government House on the south side of the city. It was the headquarters of General Odd Bull, the Norwegian chief of the United Nations Truce Supervision Organization. Surrounded by seven hundred acres, it would give Hussein easy access for his Patton tanks to invade Israeli Jerusalem.

An hour later Dayan gave the signal for Israeli troops to secure Government House. The Jerusalem Brigade drove the Jordanians from their objective and even farther south from "The Bell," a series of deep ditches used as protection from enemy gunfire. By midnight the brigade had accomplished its mission with the loss of only eight men.

About the time Dayan had ordered the Jerusalem Brigade to attack, Uzi Narkiss issued the command to Uri Ben-Ari, leader of the Harel Mechanized Brigade—tanks and motorized infantry—to take the ridges north of the corridor. He was then to intercept Jordanian tank columns advancing on Jerusalem south through Ramallah. Ben-Ari's men and tanks moved into the Jerusalem corridor. He began to send units into the ridges controlled by the Jordanians.

Ben-Ari chose four separate routes to ensure that at least one column would break through and reach the objective—Tel el-Ful. It was the strategic point where the roads south from Ramallah and west from Jericho meet to form one road into Jerusalem. The main obstacles to their advance were

Jordanian troops and a minefield that stretched the entire length of the border in the area. The ground had been mined for so long no one knew where the mines were located. Sadly, Uri Ben-Ari and his troops would find many of them before the battle ended.

At five o'clock in the morning the command was given to commence firing. Israeli tanks—supported by jet fighter-bomber attacks—blasted the Jordanian bunkers blocking their way. The infantry moved forward while engineers set out to find the mines, equipped only with bayonets, cleaning rods, and other improvised equipment. Many of the men lost legs that grisly day.

As dawn crept over the battlefield, Ben-Ari's units had managed to reach the outskirts of Tel el-Ful. They had only four Sherman tanks, several half-tracks, and a few vehicles from the reconnaissance unit. They soon spotted three Patton tanks moving toward them from Jericho and opened fire. They scored direct hits, but to their astonishment the 75mm shells bounced off the Pattons' heavy armor plate. Supplied with 90mm guns, the tanks returned fire and scored a direct hit on one of the Israeli tanks. With its commander wounded and its main gun destroyed, the Sherman withdrew. The firing pin on the second Sherman cannon broke, leaving two Israeli tanks to level ineffective fire at the advancing Jordanian Pattons. If the three Jordanian tanks kept coming, there was little the Israelis could do to stop them. Lying just behind the advancing Patton tanks were twenty more awaiting orders of engagement.

Suddenly, the Jordanian tanks began to turn and withdraw behind Tel el-Ful. The cessation of fire gave the Israelis an opportunity to crew the tank with the damaged gun and rejoin the operative Sherman tanks. Soon thereafter, Patton tanks came from behind Tel el-Ful to rejoin the fray. The Israelis resumed firing only to again see their shells bounce off the Jordanian tanks.

Sitting in the turret of the tank with the disabled cannon was Sergeant Mordechai Eitan. He had been studying the Patton tanks through his binoculars when he spotted metal containers mounted on the backs of the Jordanian tanks. Could they be auxiliary fuel tanks?

There was only one way to find out: He cocked the heavy machine gun on his tank's turret and opened fire on the containers. A direct hit on one of the containers caused the Patton to burst into flames. The terrified crew of the tank beside it bailed out and ran for their lives. One Jordanian tank kept coming toward the Israeli line. Just as its commander broke through, Israeli air support arrived and directed a well-aimed round at the Patton tank. The remainder of the Jordanians turned and headed back to Jericho. Ben-Ari's troops had secured the road to Jerusalem and firmly blocked it.

In Tel Aviv, Colonel Mordechai Gur and his 55th Paratroop Brigade had been scheduled for deployment in the Sinai. Things were going so well there, however, that the high command offered their services to Narkiss. Colonel Gur and his staff arrived in Jerusalem a few hours ahead of their paratroopers. The greatest difficulty facing Gur's plan to penetrate the Green line—as the border with Jordan was called—was whether to attack at night or wait for dawn. Since Dayan had ruled out air support because of the holy sites, it made little sense to wait for daylight; launching a night attack might even give the Israelis an advantage.

The battle for Jerusalem was bloody and costly. The Jordanians had withdrawn to entrenched positions on Ammunition Hill. Here, the Israelis encountered massive resistance. In the early morning hours, two prongs of the paratrooper attack crossed just north of the Mandelbaum Gate. One unit headed toward the Old City, the other toward several Arab strongholds. Both groups encountered fierce street-to-street combat. By noon, however, Jordanian resistance had ended.

Perhaps the most critical struggle for Jerusalem was fought not on the battlefield but in the cabinet of Prime Minister Eshkol. Defense Minister Moshe Dayan and Menachem Begin were in favor of surrounding the Old City and choking it into surrender. Others in Eshkol's cabinet were in favor of liberating all of Jerusalem. Dayan's plan remained in effect until he and Narkiss drove to Mount Scopus to survey the area. As Dayan gazed out over the Old City—Jerusalem the Golden—he realized the city had to be taken or it would be lost.

At the cabinet meeting that night, Eshkol issued orders through Chief of Staff Yitzhak Rabin to take the city. Colonel Mordechai Gur arranged for detachments to enter the Old City through its gates. The main thrust would be through the Lion's Gate opposite the Mount of Olives. Resistance was minimal. The remainder of the day was relegated to rejoicing and the costly work of eliminating the last pockets of Jordanian opposition.

At the same time the Western Wall was being liberated, columns of Israeli tanks and infantry continued pressing the Jordanians throughout Samaria and Judea—called the West Bank by Arabs. My beloved friend General Mordechai Gur, who was a 37- year-old colonel at that time, led his 55th Paratroopers Brigade to defend Jerusalem. Years later in his office in Jerusalem he told me, "On Wednesday morning, June 7th, I and my paratroopers stormed into the Old City and advanced on the Temple Mount. I wept as I shouted over my communications system, 'The Temple Mount is in our hands!'"[21]

Gur continued to tell me of his experience:

> I had long looked forward to liberating Jerusalem as something sublime. For me it was the culmination of my most personal goals as a youngster, as a Jew, and as a soldier. To me, the Temple Mount was more important than the Western Wall because the Temple was the center of religion, the center of tradition. It was also the center of the kingdom, of the state, of all our hopes. The day we took it, I wrote in my diary, "What will my family say when they hear we again liberated Jerusalem just as the Maccabees once did?" Jerusalem has only been a functioning capital when the Jews have ruled it.[22]

By sundown on June 7, the Israelis had reached the Jordan River. King Hussein had paid dearly for his gamble on the Egyptian propaganda. He suffered over six thousand casualties—dead, wounded, missing—in his army. His air force had been decimated and half his tanks destroyed. He had lost his dynasty's last claim to the Islamic holy places. He had, moreover, lost more than that. The West Bank had been his richest agricultural land. Tourist income from Jerusalem and Bethlehem had accounted for 40 percent of

Jordan's revenue. His only consolation was that the Jews had suffered more casualties against his army (1,756) than they had in the much larger Sinai campaign (1,075). One-fourth of Israel's losses had come in Jerusalem.

Few Israelis found time for mourning. Chief Rabbi Shlomo Goren related to me:

> I managed to reach the Western Wall even before the firing had died down. Like one of Joshua's priests, I was running with the ram's horn, the shofar, in my hand. When I placed it to my lips and blew, I felt like thousands of shofars from the time of King David were blowing all at once.[23]

Jews from every nation were dancing and weeping as they touched the Western Wall. They sang, *"Yerushalayim Shel Zahav"*...Jerusalem of Gold. Prime Minister Yitzhak Rabin told me years later:

> This was the most holy day of my life. I heard rabbis crying that the Messiah was coming soon, and that ancient prophecy was fulfilled that day. You would have thought King David had returned with his harp and the Ark of the Covenant.[24]

Hardened veterans ran to touch the ancient wall, tears flowing down their faces in gratitude. "Next year, Jerusalem," was no longer a heartrending cry; it was reality. To pray at the Western Wall was no longer a yearning; it was a certainty. The Temple Mount, on which stands the Dome of the Rock, still remained closed to the Jewish people, but they could at least stretch out their fingertips and touch a portion of it.

Most importantly, Jerusalem was united and in Jewish hands. What Jehovah had sworn to Abraham centuries before had once again been confirmed:

> That in blessing I will bless thee, and in multiplying I will multiply thy seed as the stars of the heaven, and as the sand

which [is] upon the sea shore; and thy seed shall possess the
gate of his enemies...(Genesis 22:17, KJV.)

God's commanded blessing had again been spread over the city upon
which His name rests.

CHAPTER 14

SUPPORT FOR ISRAEL BRINGS BLESSINGS

"The LORD also will roar from Zion, And utter His voice from Jerusalem; The heavens and earth will shake; But the LORD will be a shelter for His people, And the strength of the children of Israel."

(JOEL 3:16, NKJV)

In one of my many discussions with Israeli Prime Minister Menachem Begin I asked:

> "How can so many deny that Jerusalem is the capital of Israel when scores of people in America and the world believe the Bible?"

Mr. Begin simply smiled that enigmatic smile of his. As we talked, I told him about a publication that had come into my possession from the Egyptian state information service. It had been printed by *al-Ahram* press in Cairo, and was titled, "Jerusalem, an Arab City." The book stated on page eight, "Jerusalem was invaded by Christian Arabs in the year 90 BC and remained under their domination until it was occupied by the Romans in the first century AD."[25]

Of course, both of us were well aware that the Arab world's claim to Jerusalem was based on misinformation. How could a state publication declare a right to Jerusalem based on the presumption that Christian Arabs had invaded Jerusalem 90 years *before* the birth of Christ? It is this type of propaganda that floods the Arab world, and which continues to feed and fuel hatred for the Jewish people.

The prime minister answered my question:

> "Being a student of the Bible, you know that almost 3,000 years ago King David united the Kingdoms of Judea and Israel. He transferred the seat of power from Hebron to Jerusalem, where he ruled for thirty-three years. He wanted to build the Temple on Mount Moriah, where Abraham had offered his son, Isaac, as a sacrifice.
>
> "David petitioned God to be allowed to build a home for Him in Jerusalem. God answered, 'You have shed much blood and have made great wars; you shall not build a house for My name, because you have shed much blood on the earth in My sight,' (I Chronicles 22:8.) God promised David a son who would follow after him as king and would build the Temple. Since then, Jerusalem has been the capital of the Jewish state…one of the oldest capital cities in the world."

The Prime Minister was aware of the detractors who refused to recognize the State of Israel, much less Jerusalem as its capital city:

> "We came to Camp David to make peace with Egypt and one of your statesmen told me that the government of the United States did not recognize Jerusalem as the capital of Israel. I answered, 'Whether you recognize or do not recognize, Jerusalem is the capital of the State of Israel.'
>
> "After the Six Day War, we liberated the eastern part of Jerusalem from Jordanian occupation. For nineteen years we could not go to the Western Wall to pray. That was the only

time since the [second] Temple had been destroyed by the Romans. Under all other regimes we were free to go to the Western Wall to pray, but the Jordanians did not allow us passage, in breach of the arms agreement.

"The Olive Mountain Cemetery in which our greatest sages are buried for centuries was completely desecrated. Monuments were destroyed and turned into floors of places which are unmentionable. I will not even use the names [latrines]. All of our synagogues were destroyed...the Jewish Quarter, which was centuries old was leveled.

"Under our jurisdiction, we reconsecrated the Olive Mountain Cemetery and everyone has access to the Holy Shrines—the Holy Sepulchre, the Church of the Nativity. A Muslim goes to a mosque to pray in absolute safety.

"Here in Jerusalem is the government, the Parliament, the president, the Supreme Court. Whoever says, either on behalf of a great power or of a small country, 'We cannot recognize Jerusalem as the capital of Israel,' my reply is always the same."

Israel is now, and always will be, the "apple of His [God's] eye," (Zechariah 2:8.) The city is God's joy and delight, His royal diadem (Isaiah 62:3), His firstborn, His chosen one, His beloved (Jeremiah 2:2, Hosea 11:1.) God says of His people, "For they shall be like the jewels of a crown" (Zechariah 9:16, NKJV.) In actuality, God has written His name in Jerusalem; it is His city.

On July 30, 1980, thirteen years after Jerusalem was reunified during the Six Day War, the Israeli Knesset voted to affirm a united Jerusalem as the capital of the State of Israel. Shortly afterward, I had the privilege of sitting down with Prime Minister Begin, the man who had become my dear friend. We talked about the vastness of the territory held by Israel's enemies. It seemed inconceivable to me that Arab countries are 650 times the size of Israel; and that by comparison, Israel is only slightly larger than the state of New Jersey. The Arab countries, on the other hand, are comparable to the

entire United States and all of Mexico and Central America combined. For
instance, in 1980:

✧ Arab dictators controlled 13,486,861 square
kilometers in the Middle East, and Israel
controlled 20,770 (Palestinefacts.org).

✧ The population of Israel is roughly 7.95 million, compared to the population of 300 million living in the surrounding Arab countries.

✧ The Arab nations are represented
by 21 separate countries.[26]

The prime minister's comments brought to mind something Moshe
Dayan said during his address to the 34th General Assembly of the United
Nations in September 1979:

"Jerusalem has known many foreign rulers during the
course of its long history, but none of them regarded it as
their capital. Only the Jewish people have always maintained
it as the sole center of its national and spiritual life. For
thousands of years Jews have prayed daily for their return
to Jerusalem, and for the past century and a half, Jerusalem
has had a continuous and uninterrupted Jewish majority."[27]

Jerusalem is the symbol of all that Israel represents in our world. Teddy
Kollek, Jerusalem's first mayor wrote:

"Jerusalem, this beautiful, golden city, is the heart and
soul of the Jewish people. One cannot live without a heart
and soul. If you want one single word to symbolize all of
Jewish history, that word is Jerusalem."[28]

Out of the long negotiations to establish a Jewish homeland a friendship
grew between Dr. Chaim Weizmann, a Jewish statesman, and Lord Balfour,

British foreign secretary. Balfour was unable to understand why the Jews were insisting they would only accept Palestine as their permanent homeland. One day Lord Balfour asked Dr. Weizmann for an explanation. "Mr. Balfour, let's suppose I propose that you replace London with Paris, would you accept?"

A surprised Balfour responded, "But, London is ours!"

Replied Weizmann, "Jerusalem was ours when London was still a swampland."[29]

The very name evokes a stirring in the heart and soul. It has been called by many names: City of God, City of David, Zion, the City of the Great King, Ariel (Lion of God), Moriah (chosen of the Lord). But only one name resonates down through the centuries—Jerusalem! David's city!

A world map drawn in 1581 has Jerusalem at its very center with the then-known continents of the world surrounding it. It resembles a ship's propeller with the shaft in the center being Jerusalem. Another analogy is of Jerusalem as the navel of the earth.

Jerusalem's history can be summed up in one word—troubled! Lying as it does between the rival empires of Egypt to the south and Syria to the north, both striving for dominance in the region, Israel has constantly been trampled by opposing armies. It has been conquered at various times by the Canaanites, Jebusites, Babylonians, Assyrians, Persians, Romans, Byzantines, Arabs, Crusaders, Ottomans, and the British. While its origins are lost in the hazy mists of antiquity, archaeological evidence of human habitation goes back some 4,000 years.

Jerusalem is first mentioned in Joshua 10:1. We read there that Adoni-Zedek was the king of Jerusalem and fought unsuccessfully against Joshua. The Israelites first occupied Jerusalem during the days of the Judges (1:21), but did not completely inhabit the city until 1049 BC when David wrested it from the Jebusites and declared it the capital city of the Jewish people.

In *Jerusalem, Sacred City of Mankind*, Teddy Kollek and Moshe Pearlman wrote:

> "The spiritual attachment of the Jews to Jerusalem has remained unbroken; it is a unique attachment. Should one

doubt that statement, he would have to look long and hard to find another relationship in history where a people, even in captivity, remained so passionately attached to a city for 3,000 years."[30]

When the Jews were driven from their land at various times, wherever they found themselves in exile, they faced toward Jerusalem when praying. Jewish synagogues faced Jerusalem. When a Jew built a house part of a wall was left unfinished to symbolize that it was only a temporary dwelling—until he could return to his permanent home, Jerusalem. Even the traditional smashing of a glass during a wedding ceremony has its roots in the Temple in Jerusalem. This act of remembering the loss at the center of Jewish festivities during the marriage feast sets "Jerusalem above [their] highest joy," (Psalm 137:6, KJV.)

When compared with the great cities of the world, Jerusalem is small. It sits alongside no great river as does London, Paris, and Rome. It boasts no port, no major industries, no known mineral wealth or even an adequate water supply. The city doesn't lie on a major thoroughfare connected to the rest of the world. Why then is Jerusalem the navel of the earth, the shaft that propels the world ever forward?

The answer can be found in its spiritual significance. Jerusalem is the home of two of the world's monotheistic faiths—Judaism and Christianity, and is claimed by a third—Islam. Biblical prophets proclaimed that from Jerusalem the Word of the Lord would go out to the world—a Word, which would change the moral standards of all mankind.

The spiritual stature of Jerusalem is echoed in its physical situation; it rests upon the Judean hills high above the surrounding countryside. Traveling to Jerusalem is always spoken of as "going up to Jerusalem." Those who leave the City of God are said to "go down"—in perhaps more than just the physical sense.

When viewing the history of Jerusalem as a whole, no other city has suffered as has David's City. At times the city has been overrun by violent assailants. It is recorded in Jeremiah that the city surrendered after suffering the horrors of starvation—and had been reduced to cannibalism (Jeremiah 19).

While Christian and Muslim claims to Jerusalem came much later, the story of the Jews in Jerusalem began three millennia ago, and has never ceased. The link of the Jewish people has been historical, religious, cultural, physical, and fundamental. It has never been voluntarily broken; any absence of the Jews from their beloved city has been the result of foreign persecution and expulsion. To the Jews alone belongs David's City, the City of God.

For the Jewish people whose cry for centuries has been, "Next year Jerusalem," it is more than a location on the map, it is not just a tourist Mecca where one can visit various holy sites; Jerusalem *is* holy. It is the essence of all for which the Jews have hoped and prayed and cried and died. It is their God-given land.

When you and I as Christians are apathetic toward God's divine plan or His eternal purpose, it means that we are rejecting our Lord's heavenly assignment to the Church. God's prophetic time clock has been set on Jerusalem time throughout history, and the spotlight of heaven is still on the Jews as His Chosen People. It began with them, and it will end with them.

We embrace the name of Christ and serve the God of Abraham, Isaac, and Jacob. We heed the warnings of the prophets Isaiah, Jeremiah, Ezekiel, Daniel, Hosea, and Joel. We sing the Psalms of King David and find hope. The mention of Jerusalem quickens our hearts, for it is our spiritual city. We support our Jewish brothers and sisters in their fight against anti-Semitism and the threat of terrorism.

God's plan is an eternal one! As Christians, we cannot afford to neglect our responsibility to stand with the House of Israel. It is as important as it is to believe the promises of God. As Christians, we are the engrafted vine; we bow before a Jewish Messiah; and what we do matters in the light of eternity.

Jerusalem is the only city for which God commands us to pray:

Pray for the peace of Jerusalem: ""May they prosper who love you," (Psalm 122:6.) It is a prayer with a promise: pray/prosper, sow/reap, bless/ be blessed. The commanded blessing in return for intercession for Jerusalem is one of peace: peace with the Creator, internal peace, peace in the midst of storms, peace forevermore. One Bible commentary interprets this verse as follows:

The essential idea is that of quietness or rest; and the meaning here is, that those who love Zion will have peace; or, that the tendency of that love is to produce peace.[31]

If you desire the blessings of peace in your home, your church, your spiritual life and love unfailing, pray for the peace of Jerusalem, the city whose name means "peace."

When you pray for Jerusalem, you are not praying for stones or dirt, you are praying for revival (2 Chronicles 7:14), and for the Lord's return. Also, you are joining our Lord, the Good Samaritan, in His ministry of love and comfort to the suffering. "Inasmuch as you did it to one of the least of these My brethren, you did it to Me," (Matthew 25:40.) Praying for the peace of Jerusalem brings a commanded blessing of peace to the intercessor.

King David explained precisely why God Almighty has instructed us to pray for the peace of Jerusalem, and has commanded a blessing upon us for doing so. The revelation is found in Psalm 122:8: "For the sake of my brethren and companions, I will now say, 'Peace be within you.'" God is telling us to pray for the peace of the inhabitants of Jerusalem. David felt that prayer needed to be offered up for all of his brothers, and friends who lived there. Prayer needs to be offered today for the House of Israel and for peace for those who reside there from the over 120 nations of the world. It is the city most targeted by terrorists, simply because of hatred for the Jewish people and the significance of Jerusalem to them. It has drawn the Jewish people of the world like a prophetic magnet—those who have prayed, "Next year in Jerusalem."

In Psalm 122:9, David's revelation says, "Because of the house of the LORD our God I will seek your good." When we pray for the peace of Jerusalem, we are ultimately praying for Satan to be bound. In Isaiah 14, Satan said he would battle God from the Temple of the Lord, on the sides of the north. When we pray for the peace of Jerusalem, we are praying for those who live there, and we are praying for the Messiah to come. The prophecies of the Bible point to the Temple of the Lord as the key flashpoint that will bring the nations of the world to Jerusalem, and result in the battle that will end Satan's reign over the earth for all eternity. It will spell his final defeat!

It is evident from Scripture that the Sovereign Lord of Creation has chosen the city of Jerusalem as His earthly capital. This decision was made by the very same God who promised to restore His covenanted Jewish people to the sacred city and surrounding land in the last days before the Second Coming. How can Christians look for and welcome Jesus' prophesied return, and not rejoice in and actively support the Jewish return that was foretold to at least partially precede it?

God described the details and boundaries of the land in Genesis 15:18-21: "On the same day the Lord made a covenant with Abram, saying: 'To your descendants I have given this land, from the river of Egypt to the great river, the River Euphrates.'" This was a royal land grant, perpetual and unconditional. Genesis 17:8: "Also I give to you and your descendants after you the land in which you are a stranger, all the land of Canaan, as an everlasting possession; and I will be their God." Genesis 28:13: "the land on which you lie I will give to you and your descendants." Abraham's title deed to the land has never been revoked, nor has Jehovah given it to anyone else.

God bestowed a commanded blessing upon Abraham and his descendants. His covenant relationship with God began because he believed. Abraham received a commanded blessing because our Lord does not lie; He is the same yesterday, today, and forever. Because of His steadfastness, the central theme of the entire Bible from Genesis to Revelation is faith, and God abundantly blesses His faithful followers.

Jerusalem has always had a distinct destiny and a matchless calling before Jehovah. The prophet Daniel referred to it as God's "holy mountain," (Daniel 9:20, NLT.) As the location chosen to build the Temple, and as the city in which Messiah will usher in his earthly kingdom Jerusalem is biblically and eternally the City of God (Psalm 46:4, NKJV.)

CHAPTER 15

ISRAEL ENJOYS BLESSINGS ABUNDANTLY

Happy are you, O Israel! Who is like you, a people saved
by the LORD, The shield of your help And the sword of your majesty!
Your enemies shall submit to you, And you shall tread down
their high places."

(DEUTERONOMY 33:29, NKJV)

Just as God blesses those who bless Israel, so He has blessed His Chosen People. Media focus on the tiny Middle Eastern country is normally consumed with the conflict between the Jews and neighbors who decry her very existence. Rather than be cowed by all the negative attention derived from international criticism, Israelis have chosen to take the high road and continue to work on inventions and discoveries that benefit the world population in general.

Jealousy could likely be the reason fundamental Islam fanatically targets not only the Jews in Israel but United States' citizens, according to noted Jewish lecturer, Irwin N. Graulich:

In addition, during that same period [1948–current], Israel totally embarrassed the entire Arab/Muslim world by defeating them economically, technologically, intellectually, culturally, religiously, medically, socially and morally. Since America's accomplishments are that much greater, it is no wonder that the Arab/Muslim nations feel totally frustrated. They subscribe to a religious belief that promises world greatness, strength and domination, while reality shows them trailing very far behind.[32]

Not only are there numerous inventive and creative people in Israel, there is a sense of generosity and compassion few of its neighbors deign to recognize and/or accept. For example, a World News article on NBC.com revealed a heartwarming story of unheralded assistance to a family in Syria:

The young girl was dying when she arrived in the land of her country's enemy. A heart condition had left the 4-year-old Syrian struggling to walk or even talk. But in Israel—a country still in a state of cease-fire with Syria after the Yom Kippur War four decades ago—she found her saviors. Admitted in early 2013 to the Wolfson Medical Center, south of Tel Aviv, she underwent life-saving surgery. The girl is now recuperating on a ward along with children from the West Bank and Gaza Strip, Sudan, Romania, China and Israel. "She would have definitely died if she wouldn't have arrived here," Ilan Cohen, one of the doctors who treated her, said. "A lot of patients arrive here from enemy countries and view Israelis as demons. They are surprised that we are human without horns on our heads," he added. "This is the first time they see Israelis without a uniform and I think it's a good surprise." Her treatment was the work of "Save a Child's Heart," an Israeli nonprofit organization started by the late Ami Cohen, who moved to Israel from the United States in 1992. He joined the staff of the Wolfson with a vision to mending children's hearts from around the world. The organization he began has since helped treat 3,200 children from 45 countries.[33]

The story went on to tell of the mother's fear of reprisal upon their return home. It seems incredible that hatred could be so strong as to fault a family for trying to save a beloved child; and yet it is. The other side of that story is the men and women who provided the techniques and services that saved the life of the young girl.

In the sixty-five-plus years since Israel was recognized as a state in the mid-1940s, amazing strides have been made in science, technology, medicine, farming, and communication thanks to the diligence of the people who live in the Holy Land.

There have been some mind-boggling discoveries in the field of medicine:

> In 1954, Ephraim Frei discovered the effects of magnetism on the human body. His exploration led to the advancement of the T-scan system, a breakthrough in the advancement for detecting breast cancer.
>
> In 1956, Professor Leo Sachs developed amniocentesis to uncover the benefits of examining amniotic fluid in the diagnosis of prenatal anomalies. It has become a major obstetrics tool in aiding pregnant women and their unborn babies. In 1963, Sachs became the first to grow lab-bred blood cells, a tool used to help chemotherapy patients.
>
> Ada Yonath, awarded the Nobel Prize in Chemistry in 2009, laid the groundwork for the advent of drugs that are used to treat some strains of leukemia, glaucoma and HIV, as well as antipsychotic and antidepressant medicines.

Added to these inspired and ingenious men and women are Meir Wilcheck, the discoverer of blood detoxification; Elli Canaani, a drug to treat chronic myelogenous leukemia; Avram Hershko and Aaron Ciechanover, cellular research to better determine the cause of ailments such as cervical cancer and cystic fibrosis; and, the creation of Copaxone, the only non-interferon treatment for multiple sclerosis. These are only a few of the many advancements in detection and management of a myriad of diseases and serious health conditions. Amazing and innovative techniques have originated in the field of spinal surgery, treatment of Parkinson's disease, tumor and small bowel (Pillcam) imaging, in first-aid in the form of innovative field dressings that are now the global standard, the Lubocollar used to treat trauma patients world-wide, helping paraplegics walk, treating diabetes, artificial limb improve-ments, and more.

Israel has silently and steadily blossomed into an enthusiastic and impres-sive proving ground for entrepreneurs and inventors. In the field of technol-ogy, just a few examples are:

> The Uzi machine gun developed by Major Uzi Gaf; mil-lions are in use globally.
> The WEIZAC computer introduced by the Weizmann Institute in 1955 was one of the first, "large-scale stored pro-gram computers in the world."[34]
> A solar energy system that today is used to power the majority of hot water heaters worldwide.

We could also include color holograms, desalination processes, drone aircraft, computer processors, digital information sharing, terrorist detectors, and thousands of other technology-based products.[35]

Farmers worldwide have enjoyed the benefits of advances such as the super cucumber and disease resistant potatoes, improved food storage systems, drip irrigation, extracting water from the air, bee preservation, advanced fish farming, water purification, and more ecologically-friendly food packaging.

Add to this list baby monitors, instant messaging, office equipment, the Babylon computer dictionary, flash drives, micro-computers, miniature video cameras, computer chips, advances in airport safety, and missile defense sys-tems. It is an incredible list, a testament to the ingenuity and inventiveness of the Jewish people.

Many of these inventions capture Nobel prizes for those responsible, but the awards are not confined to science and technology. Now, they are shared by authors, poets, mathematicians, peacemakers and economists.

It is amazing to discover that 22 percent of all individual Nobel Prize

winners worldwide between its inception in 1901 and 2012 have been of
Jewish descent. That alone is an amazing number to contemplate.

Two Jewish laureates were honored after having endured incarceration
in concentration camps during the Holocaust: Imre Kertész and Elie Wiesel.
At the age of 14, Kertész was rounded up with other Hungarian Jews and sent
first to Auschwitz, and then to Buchenwald. He was a prolific writer whose
best-known novel, *Fatelessness* (*Sorstalanság*), unveiled the experiences of a
teenage boy who was sent to the camps at Auchwitz, Buchenwald, and Zeitz.
He was awarded the Prize in 2002 "for writing that upholds the fragile experience of the individual against the barbaric arbitrariness of history."[36]

Elie Wiesel, who was also sent to Auschwitz, Buna, and Buchenwald during World War II, received the Nobel Prize in 1986. The committee characterized him as a "messenger to mankind," stating that through his struggle to
come to terms with "his own personal experience of total humiliation and of
the utter contempt for humanity shown in Hitler's death camps", as well as his
"practical work in the cause of peace", Wiesel had delivered a powerful message "of peace, atonement and human dignity" to humanity.[37]

In 2009, I was invited to speak at a communications and law conference
held at Ariel University in Israel. It was my distinct privilege to meet Nobel
Laureate, Professor Robert Aumann of Hebrew University, and founder of the
Game Theory Society. I had been asked to attend the conference by my good
friend, the late Ron Nachman, mayor of the city of Ariel, and was able to see
firsthand the genius of the professor.

Born in Germany, Aumann and his family escaped just fourteen days
before the ravages of *Kristallnacht*, a series of coordinated attacks against Jews
in Nazi Germany and parts of Austria. In a 2005 Jerusalem Post article, jour-
nalist Hilary Leila Krieger wrote:

> The year was 1938 and the Aumanns desperately wanted
> to leave their native Germany. Salvation dangled in the form
> of US visas, available for passport holders who swore they
> wouldn't be a burden on their new country and passed a
> test of basic American terms and concepts. Robert "Yis-
> rael" Aumann saw his parents studying hard and thought he

should do likewise. After his parents passed the exam, his mother confided in the consular official that her son had also prepared very diligently and would like to be presented with a test question. The consul leaned over to the eight-year-old and asked him to name the president of the United States - at the time Franklin D. Roosevelt. Aumann answered enthusiastically: "Rosenfeld!" The consul burst out laughing. He also granted the boy a visa. The qualities Aumann displayed at a ripe age - a propensity for hard work, a fierce intellect and a commitment to Jewish values - and has continued to exhibit throughout adulthood, earned him this year's Nobel prize in economics.[38]

When presented with the Nobel Prize in 2005, the Professor titled his acceptance speech "War and Peace." He said to the assembled audience:

"Simplistic peacemaking can cause war, while arms race, credible war threats and mutually assured destruction can reliably prevent war."[39]

Ernest Hemingway wrote: The world breaks everyone, and afterward, some are strong at the broken places.[40] Adversity has forged a people of great strength, resiliency, insight, and intelligence. As the psalmist wrote in Psalm 115:12, ESV: "The LORD has remembered us; he will bless us; he will bless the house of Israel..."

The list of brilliant men and women who have sprung from Abraham, Isaac, and Jacob is long and impressive: Nelly Sachs, Shmuel Yosef Agnon, Saul Bellow, Ada Yonath, Isaac Bashevis Singer, Dan Shechtman, Menachem Begin, Yitzhak Rabin, and Shimon Peres.

Brilliance, tenacity, and determination are not confined to Nobel Prize winners. It is found in all men and women who are determined to work hard, teach their children, bless their neighbors, feed the hungry, extend a helping hand to those in need, and build on the foundations of the past to reap the commanded blessings of Jehovah, He who blesses the House of Israel.

CHAPTER 16

BLESSED WITH REUNIFICATION & RESTORATION

"and those the LORD *has rescued will return. They will enter Zion
with singing; everlasting joy will crown their heads. Gladness and
joy will overtake them, and sorrow and sighing will flee away."*

(ISAIAH 35:10, NIV)

Through the centuries, the Holy City has been besieged by nations,
trampled underfoot and leveled to the ground and still the cry
has rung out, "Next year, Jerusalem." The Jewish people have been broken time and again, yet have returned even stronger and more capable. A river of tears has flowed down through the ages as God's people prayed for deliverance. From the frozen wastelands of Siberia, and
from the hot sands of the Ethiopian desert, they have cried out. Jews
marked for destruction in Treblinka...Bergen-Belsen...and in the ovens
of Auschwitz...Ravensbruck...Buchenwald, yearned for their ancient
homeland.

Why? Perhaps Pope John Paul II said it best:

"For the Jews, Jerusalem is the object of a profound love,
full of the footprints of many generations and a wealth of
memories from the time of David, who chose it as his capital, and of Solomon, who built the Temple. Since then, their
eyes have been set upon it...day after day they focus on it as
a symbol of their nation."[41]

For nineteen long years, from 1948 to 1967, the Jewish people could
only stand and gaze longingly at the Holy City and the distant site of the
Temple Mount in East Jerusalem. The Western Wall Square was piled high
with garbage. A road divided the Jewish cemetery on the Mount of Olives.
Conditions in Jerusalem were deplorable, even by medieval standards.

Jews were barred from worshiping at the Western Wall, and the Jewish
quarter in the old city was destroyed. Tombstones were carried away to be
used as building blocks for latrines and floors. Synagogues—fifty-eight in
all—were decimated or desecrated. The Arab occupiers tried to destroy any
trace of a Jewish presence in East Jerusalem. Still the cry rang out, "Next
year, Jerusalem."

And then, miraculously, the cry was answered for the Jews living in
Israel.

On May 16, 1967, the day began ominously: Egypt's President Gamal
Abdul Nasser was determined to stop that cry once and for all time. Egyptian
troops moved into the Sinai, and UN troops were ordered to leave. Nasser's
next move was an attempt to starve the Jewish people out with a blockade of
the Gulf of Aqaba. Jordan, Syria and the Arab League soon joined Egypt. The
Arab world had aligned itself against tiny Israel...and God!

And Almighty God roared through the heavens, "ENOUGH!"

On June 5, 1967 after months of saber rattling by Egypt, Syria, and
Jordan, Israeli military strategists unfolded a brilliant defense plan. Early
that day almost the entire Israeli Air Force took off for Cairo launching a
lightning attack against the Arab states. Israeli fighter pilots destroyed 304
Egyptian Air Force planes, 53 Syrian jets, and 28 Jordanian planes. Could
this have been what Isaiah saw when he prophesied?

"As birds flying, so will the LORD of hosts defend Jerusalem; defending also he will deliver it, and passing over he will preserve it," (Isaiah 31:5, KJV.)

Less than two hours later, its planes returned to home base having destroyed three hundred of Egypt's jets on the ground. In three days of ground fighting, the Israeli Defense Force overcame Jordanian and Egyptian forces, and the battle moved northward to the Golan Heights.

On June 7 the IDF moved into Jerusalem and recaptured the Old City, including the Western Wall. On June 9, Israeli forces broke through Syrian lines and secured that area. Since then the question of who owns Jerusalem—biblically, historically, and legally—has been asked repeatedly. The city belongs to the Jewish people, and has since the time of King David.

In approximately 1,000 BC King David defeated the Jebusites and reigned for thirty-three years in Jerusalem. After David's death, Solomon ascended the throne. When he died the land was divided into two kingdoms—Israel to the north and Judah in the south. Jerusalem became the capital of Judah. Then began a succession of Jewish rulers, until the day Nebuchadnezzar besieged and destroyed Jerusalem, leaving only a remnant of Jewish people. This was the beginning of sorrows that has continued down through the ages and persists today.

Adolf Hitler's determination to destroy the Jewish people during World War II resulted in the murder of six million Jews; European Jews pled with many nations to grant them asylum, but their pleas fell on deaf ears. Many more yearned to return to their homeland. In the midst of incredible persecution and suffering, Ezekiel's words beckoned to all and since 1948 were finally fulfilled:

For I will take you from among the nations, gather you out of all countries, and bring you into your own land, (Ezekiel 36:24, KJV.)

During my close relationship with Prime Minister Menachem Begin, our talks often centered on Jerusalem. To him it seemed unfair that, while every country in the world was free to choose its own capital, Israel was not.

He reflected on how Israel had fought to reunite Jerusalem and make it a city whose holy sites were available to everyone. He related to me an exasperating discussion he had had with President Jimmy Carter. According to Carter, his "government did not recognize Jerusalem as the capital of Israel." Begin said, "Here in Jerusalem is the [government]. Whoever says we don't recognize Jerusalem as the capital of Israel, my reply is always, 'Excuse me, sir, but we don't recognize your non-recognition.'"

Maps in Muslim countries show Israel simply as "Palestine" or unnamed. She is surrounded by hostile Muslim countries with a land mass 640 times her size, yet some thirteen million Jews worldwide are constantly charged with being accountable for the frustrations of the three hundred million Arabs in the region.

On October 6, 1973, Yom Kippur, the holiest day of the Jewish year, the Arab coalition struck Israel with a sneak attack in the hope of finally driving the Jews into the Mediterranean. When the war began, Israel was tragically caught off-guard. Most of its citizen army were in synagogues, its national radio was off the air, and people were enjoying a restful day of reflection and prayer. Israel had no immediate response to the coordinated attacks by Egypt and Syria. Israeli intelligence had not seen the assault coming, and her military was ill prepared for war.

At the outset of hostilities, Egypt attacked across the Suez Canal. The battle raged for three days, and then the Egyptian army established entrenchments which resulted in an impasse. On the northern border, Syria launched an offensive at the Golan Heights. The initial assault was successful but quickly lost momentum. By the third day of fighting Israel had lost several thousand soldiers (more Israeli causalities were lost in the first day than in the entire Six-Day War), forty-nine planes, one-third (more than five hundred) of her tank force, and a good chunk of the buffer lands gained in the Six-Day War. The Israelis seemed to be again on the brink of a holocaust.

On the fourth day of the war, in an act of desperation, Prime Minister Golda Meir opened up three nuclear silos and pointed the missiles toward

Egyptian and Syrian military headquarters near Cairo and Damascus. Army chief of staff Moshe Dayan was reported to have said, "This is the end of the Third Temple," in one of the crucial meetings. Later he told the press, "The situation is desperate. Everything is lost. We must withdraw."[42]

At that time Richard Nixon sat in the Oval Office. Earlier in his presidency, "Nixon made it clear he believed warfare was inevitable in the Middle East, a war that could spread and precipitate World War III, with the United States and the Soviet Union squaring off against each other."[43]

Nixon was staring down the barrel of that war, so he authorized Secretary of State Henry Kissinger to put every American plane that could fly in the air to transport all available conventional arms to Israel. The supply to defend Israel was larger than the Berlin airlift that had followed World War II and literally turned the tide of the war, saving Israel from extermination and the world from nuclear war. Nixon carried President Kennedy's agreement to militarily support Israel to the next logical level—a full military alliance.

The IDF launched a counter-offensive within the week and drove the Syrians to within twenty-five miles of Damascus. Trying to aid the Syrians, the Egyptian army went on the offensive all to no avail. Israeli troops crossed the Suez Canal and encompassed the Egyptian Third Army. When the Soviets realized what was happening, they scrambled to further assist Egypt and Syria. The Soviet threat was so real Nixon feared direct conflict with the U.S.S.R. and elevated all military personnel worldwide to DefCon III, meaning increased readiness that war was likely. However, a ceasefire was finally worked out between the U.S. and the U.S.S.R., adopted by all parties involved, and the Yom Kippur War was ended.

I've heard it said that God plus one is a majority...and this certainly proved to be true on June 7, 1967, and again in 1973 during the Yom Kippur War. The truth is that GOD is a majority, and we are the ones who are blessed when we prove him. Malachi 3:10 says:

> "...and prove me now herewith, saith Jehovah of hosts, if
> I will not open you the windows of heaven, and pour you out
> a blessing, that there shall not be room enough to receive it."

CHAPTER 17

FORFEITING THE COMMANDED BLESSING

I will bless those who bless you, And I will curse him who curses you;
And in you all the families of the earth shall be blessed."

(GENESIS 12:3, NKJV)

The prophet Micah foretold that Jerusalem would become the most important religious site globally. In Micah 4:1, he predicted:

> In the last days, the mountain of the LORD's house will
> be the highest of all— the most important place on earth. It
> will be raised above the other hills, and people from all over
> the world will stream there to worship, (Micah 4:1, NLT.)

Prophecy was not given to us in Scripture just so we would know beforehand what will happen; it was given so that we could understand our times, and be a part of God's plan for the ages.

Another vital scripture came from Zechariah, who boldly prophesied in the midst of the dispersion of the Jewish people that one day they would return to Jerusalem:

This is what the LORD Almighty says: "I will save my people from the countries of the east and the west. I will bring them back to live in Jerusalem; they will be my people, and I will be faithful and righteous to them as their God," (Zechariah 8:7–8, NIV.)

The prophet Zechariah spoke of Jerusalem as an "immovable rock":

On that day I will make Jerusalem an immovable rock. All the nations will gather against it to try to move it, but they will only hurt themselves, (Zechariah 12:3, NLT.)

Through the ages, nation after nation, tormentor after tyrant, dictator after despot has discovered that he may trifle with Jerusalem, but eventually God will draw a line. He will say, "This far and no farther." No one has been exempted from Jehovah's final determination.

Throughout her history, Jerusalem has been razed twice—by the Babylonians and the Romans—besieged 23 times, attacked 52 times, and captured and recaptured 44 times.[44] The nations that ransacked, burned, leveled, and otherwise tried to obliterate the Jewish people all failed miserably. We have only to examine history to ascertain that remnants of those once-great empires are now dust and ashes.

For example, in 332 BC Alexander the Great captured Jerusalem. At the height of his conquests, Alexander's empire covered 5.2 million square miles. Today it is non-existent. In 323 BC he fell ill in Nebuchadnezzar's temple in Babylon and died an ignominious and painful death. His empire fragmented after his death and the followers of Ptolemy in Egypt and then the Seleucids of Syria ruled over Jerusalem. The Jews, horrified by the desecration of the Temple under the Seleucid ruler, Antiochus IV, staged a revolt and regained independence under the Hasmonean Dynasty. It lasted for one hundred years, until Pompey established Roman rule in the city. The Holy Roman Empire covered an expanse of 1,000,000 square kilometers. The Holy Roman Empire collapsed after the Temple was destroyed and Jerusalem leveled. Today Italy covers 294,020 square kilometers, a mere shadow of the former Empire.

The British, who ruled over Palestine and Jerusalem following World War I, boasted that the sun never set on the British Empire. Indeed, one-fifth of the world's population was under its rule. However, after turning away Jews from both Britain and Palestine when they fled Hitler's gas chambers, and after arming Arabs to fight against them in Palestine, it quickly began to disintegrate. Gone are the days when the empire stretched from India to Canada and from Australia to Africa. Reaching a size of 33,700,000 square kilometers, the Empire spanned Africa, North and South America, Europe, Asia, Australia, and Antarctica. Great Britain today is comprised of just fourteen territories, consisting of a number of islands.

In 1517, the Ottoman ruler's conquest of Jerusalem and the land of Palestine saw it divided and ruled from Istanbul, Turkey. Initially, under the Turks, there were approximately one thousand Jewish families in Jerusalem, Shechem, Gaza, Hebron and villages in the Galilee. Those men and women were the offspring of ancestors who had never left their homeland. Some had emigrated from Northern Africa and Europe. That number grew to as many as 10,000 under Sultan Suleiman the Magnificent. With his death in 1566, conditions in Palestine began to decline, the country neglected, and much of it in the grasp of absentee landowners. It was leased to tenant farmers who were forced to pay a commanding tax on each parcel of agricultural land. The mighty forests of the Galilee and Carmel were stripped bare, and the land was overtaken by swamp and desert—a vast difference compared to the land of Israel today.

The land and its inhabitants continued to suffer until the 19th century when the Ottoman Empire began to decline. Its end signaled the beginning of *aliyah*, the return of the Jews to their homeland. At its most magnificent, the empire covered 10,450,000 square kilometers; today Turkey is comprised of approximately 780,580 square kilometers.

Now the question: Does God curse those who scheme against the city He calls His own? The answer is quite evident as history records. The Egyptians persecuted the Children of Israel during their sojourn in that country. God used mighty miracles in order to free His people; Egypt experienced judgments never before seen. Frogs, gnats, flies and locusts overran the land; hailstones so large fell that people and cattle caught out in the open were killed; the Nile—the source of life in the desert land—turned to blood. Darkness covered Egypt, and then the firstborn—from the eldest to the youngest—in every Egyptian household was taken as the death angel passed over the land. The Pharaoh who tormented the Jews and ultimately drove them from the land was forced to watch in horror as his army drowned beneath the waters of the Red Sea.

The harshest and coursest of people, the Assyrians, ravaged the land of Israel and destroyed all but Jerusalem and the 46 fortified cities in the land. Assyrian King Sennacherib wrote in his own journal:

> "Because Hezekiah, king of Judah, would not submit to my yoke, I came up against him, and by force of arms and by the might of my power I took forty-six of his strong fenced cities; and of the smaller towns which were scattered about, I took and plundered a countless number. From these places I took and carried off 200,156 persons, old and young, male and female, together with horses and mules, asses and camels, oxen and sheep, a countless multitude; and Hezekiah himself I shut up in Jerusalem, his capital city, like a bird in a cage, building towers round the city to hem him in, and raising banks of earth against the gates, so as to prevent escape...Then upon Hezekiah there fell the fear of the power of my arms, and he sent out to me the chiefs and the elders of Jerusalem with 30 talents of gold and 800 talents of silver, and divers treasures, a rich and immense booty... All these things were brought to me at Nineveh, the seat of my government."[45]

Ultimately Assyria vanished from the pages of history, and no trace is left of the crude nation.

In chapter 3, verses 2-3, 5-6, and 19 (NLT), the prophet Joel outlined at least six reasons that God would judge the nations. They are directly connected to the nation of Israel and the Jewish people:

> I will gather the armies of the world into the valley of Jehoshaphat. There I will judge them for harming my people, my special possession, [1] for scattering my people among the nations, [2] and for dividing up my land. They threw dice to decide [3] which of my people would be their slaves. [4] They traded boys to obtain prostitutes and sold girls for enough wine to get drunk. You have [5] taken my silver and gold and all my precious treasures, and have carried them off to your pagan temples. You have sold the people of Judah and Jerusalem to the Greeks, so they could take them far from their homeland.... But Egypt will become a wasteland and Edom will become a wilderness, [6] because they attacked the people of Judah and killed innocent people in their land.

The carnage described in the verses from Joel has been heaped upon the Jewish people from century to century.

About 1465 B.C. two other men—one a king the other a prophet—stood on an outcropping of rock looking out over the valley below. The smell of blood and burned animals from sacrifices to Baal permeated the air around them. On the plain below, stretching as far as the eye could see, were the children of Israel miraculously delivered from Egypt.

Frightened to death of them, King Balak had hired his best diviner, Balaam, to curse Israel. Amazingly, the only words that would come from Balaam's mouth were words of blessing. No matter how hard the false prophet tried, he could not curse Israel.

For forty years God had seasoned the younger generation of the children of Israel in the desert of adversity. Now all the older, unbelieving generation that He had rescued from the hands of Pharaoh had died—except for Joshua, Caleb, and Moses. God took Moses to the top of Mount Pisgah and showed him all the land He was giving the Israelites. It was a land flowing with milk and honey, the land of blessing. He assured Moses that His people were now in the hands of a capable leader, Joshua, who would lead the fight against the inhabitants of Canaan and possess all He had given them.

When Balak, the king of Moab, heard the stories of how the Amorites and King Bashan had fallen before the onslaught of the children of Israel, he determined that it must have been by magic. Balak concluded that if he were to defeat this ragtag army, he would need a magic spell stronger than the one the Israelites had used for their victories. He immediately sent an envoy to recruit the greatest magician in his realm, Balaam. Balak's battle strategy was to have Balaam curse the armies of Israel. Now the two men stood, heads together, trying to determine how best to curse God's chosen people.

When Balak sent for Balaam, something interesting happened. God warned Balaam not to proceed with the plan to curse the Israelites, so Balaam refused to go to Balak. When Balak sent princes to plead with Balaam to come, God told Balaam he could go, but he should only speak what He told him to speak. However, when Balaam got up the next morning and went with the princes, God was angry with him because his motivation was not to obey God but to gain wealth. Balaam thought he could act like he was obeying God, and when he got to Balak he could curse Israel and become a rich man. God saw the wickedness in Balaam's heart and sent an angel to stop him.

As Balaam set out with the princes, his donkey saw the Angel of the Lord standing, sword drawn, in the path. Frightened, she veered off into the field. Balaam struck the donkey and she returned to the path, where she saw the Angel again and lurched into a boulder. Balaam's foot was crushed, and he struck the donkey again. At that point she collapsed in the road at the feet of the Angel, and spoke to Balaam, "Am I not your donkey on which you have ridden, ever since I became yours, to this day? Was I ever disposed to do this to you?" (Numbers 22:30, NIV).

When Balaam answered no, the Angel of the Lord revealed himself to Balaam and said, "Go with the men: but speak only what I tell you," (Numbers 22:35).

Once in the presence of Balak, Balaam joined him in making a sacrifice to Baal. Obviously, his heart was not after God. He then went aside to a solitary place hoping to hear the curse that he was to pronounce upon the Israelites. God met him and put a word in his mouth, but it was not the word King Balak wanted to hear:

> How can I curse those whom God has not cursed? How can I denounce those whom the LORD has not denounced? From the rocky peaks I see them, from the heights I view them. I see a people who live apart and do not consider themselves one of the nations. Who can count the dust of Jacob or number even a fourth of Israel? Let me die the death of the righteous, and may my final end be like theirs!" (Numbers 23:8-10, NIV.)

Balak was livid. How dare this mere mortal praise Israel rather than curse them as he had ordered? Balaam replied:

> "Must I not speak what the LORD PUTS IN MY MOUTH?" (Numbers 23:12, NIV.)

Balak offered a second round of sacrifices to Baal while Balaam waited for the word of the LORD to curse Israel. Again, only blessing poured from his mouth:

> "God is not human, that he should lie, not a human being, that he should change his mind. Does he speak and then not act? Does he promise and not fulfill? "The people rise like a lioness; they rouse themselves like a lion that does not rest till it devours its prey and drinks the blood of its victims," (Numbers 23:19, 24, NIV.)

Before heading home from his failed attempt to curse the children of Israel, Balaam took his last look at the camp of the Israelites. He proclaimed:

"How beautiful are your tents, Jacob, your dwelling places, Israel! "Like valleys they spread out, like gardens beside a river, like aloes planted by the LORD, LIKE CEDARS BESIDE THE WATERS. Water will flow from their buckets; their seed will have abundant water.

"Their king will be greater than Agag; their kingdom will be exalted.

"God brought them out of Egypt; they have the strength of a wild ox. They devour hostile nations and break their bones in pieces; with their arrows they pierce them. Like a lion they crouch and lie down, like a lioness—who dares to rouse them?

"May those who bless you be blessed and those who curse you be cursed!" (Numbers 24:5-9, NIV)

He could very well have ended his association with Balak by saying, "I should have listened to the donkey!"

This is just an overview of how nations have come against Israel and attempted to curse her from the beginning of her existence. Yet, like the Phoenix, she has risen from the ashes each time. Not one ruler who ordered the destruction of Jerusalem survived. Nebuchadnezzar conquered Jerusalem in 586 B.C. and was doomed to live as a beast of the field for seven, terrifying years. He was restored to sanity when he recognized the God of the Israelites (Daniel 4:34, 37). His kingdom of Babylon was conquered by Cyrus the Great, a friend to the Jews, who allowed them to rebuild their Temple.

Although the Temple was destroyed by the Romans in 70 AD, today Jerusalem stands as a testimony to the determination and courage of the Jewish people. Our question is: Does America stand with or against Jerusalem and the nation of Israel?

God said He would bless Abraham's friends. He vowed to be a friend to Abraham's friends and to consider any benevolence as if it were a kindness to Him. No act of kindness, not even a cup of cold water, would be overlooked. Jesus extended that covenant to His followers in Mark 9:41, NKJV: "For whoever gives you a cup of water to drink in My name, because you belong to Christ, assuredly, I say to you, he will by no means lose his reward."

James 2:23, NKJV, reveals the extent of God's covenant with Abraham:

> And the Scripture was fulfilled which says, "Abraham believed God, and it was accounted to him for righteousness." And he was called the friend of God.

Would it not be the highest accolade to be called the friend of God? Abraham became known as the father of many nations and the father of the Christian faith. God has, indeed, made his name great because of his faithfulness.

God also promised Abraham that when threatened by enemies, He would provide a way of escape. There are those who continue to curse the descendants of Abraham's son Isaac. It is not by accident that the promise to curse is upon the individual: "I will bless *them...*I will curse *him*." Their futile curses against Abraham were nullified by God's blessings upon him and his descendants.

While God's blessings rain on the just and unjust (Matthew 5:45), His curses are reserved for the perpetrator alone. Each man must stand before God, the righteous Judge, and give account for his deeds and actions. If we bless God's Chosen People, not only are we blessed, but our families will be blessed. If we curse His people, we alone will stand before God in judgment. It is an individual choice.

I would much rather stand with the Jewish people and be among the blessed of the Earth. In Psalm 128:5, NJKV, the Psalmist wrote:

> "The LORD bless you out of Zion, And may you see the good of Jerusalem All the days of your life."

Today, the United Nations continues to put increased pressure upon the Jews in Israel. The nations of the world who choose not to support Israel should be extremely cautions: God will judge. He has said, "I will curse him that curses thee."

Hebrew writer Israel Matzav wrote about blessing and cursing:

> One need not be a Jew or Christian or even believe in
> God to appreciate that this verse is as accurate a prediction
> as humanity has ever been given by the ancient world. The
> Jewish people have suffered longer and more horribly than
> any other living people. But they are still around. Its historic
> enemies are all gone. Those that cursed the Jews were indeed
> cursed....Those who curse the Jews still seem to be cursed.
> The most benighted civilization today is the Arab world.
> One could make a plausible case that the Arab world's pre-
> occupation with Jew-hatred and destroying Israel is a deci-
> sive factor in its failure to progress. The day the Arab world
> makes peace with the existence of the tiny Jewish state in
> its midst, the Arab world will begin its ascent. The converse
> is what worries tens of millions of Americans — the day
> America abandons Israel, America will begin its descent.[46]

Every nation in history that has lifted a hand against Israel has been
cursed. And every nation that has blessed them has been blessed. "For he
who touches you touches the apple of His eye" (Zechariah 2:8). So what can
you and I do to bless Israel? Prayer is the most powerful weapon in Heaven's
arsenal, and brings with it a promise of the blessings of God.

Just ask Esther if prayer changes things. She came to the king in fear for
her life but left with supernatural favor. She came with poverty but left with
prosperity. She came in despair but left highly favored. She came representing a people who were marked for destruction and left the king's presence
with a way of escape for her Jewish people.

Daniel engaged in intercession in chapter 10 and changed nations. For
twenty-one days, the prophet had immersed himself in prayer. As he sought
the face of God, an angel appeared to him. The angel had startling news
for him and for those of us who have prayed earnestly and diligently. The
"prince of Persia," apparently one of Lucifer's fallen angels, had hindered the
answer to Daniel's prayer. Why is it important to know this? Persistence in

prayer pays dividends! Had Daniel not continued to intercede until the battle in the heavenlies was won, his prayers would not have been answered.

King Hezekiah was faced, as Israel is today, with the threat of annihilation. The king of Assyria made the unfortunate mistake of thinking that Hezekiah trusted in horses, chariots, and his alliance with Egypt. Using the "town crier" method of communication, the commander-in-chief of the Assyrian army stood in the midst of the town square and taunted Hezekiah. He proclaimed that *Yahweh* himself had sent the Assyrians to defeat Judah.

When the king's threats were delivered to Hezekiah in the form of a written dispatch, he did the one most important thing he could have done… he went to the Temple, spread the letter on the altar, and prostrated himself before God. Hezekiah prayed:

> "Now therefore, O LORD our God, I pray, save us from his
> hand, that all the kingdoms of the earth may know that You
> are the LORD God, You alone" (II Kings 19:19, NJKV.)

God spoke the answer to Hezekiah's prayer through the prophet Isaiah: "For I will defend this city, to save it For My own sake and for My servant David's sake" (Isaiah 37:35, NKJV.) The king could have heard no sweeter words than the promise that God would defend the City of David.

Nehemiah also knew the power of prayer and intercession. He had been exiled to Babylon and elevated to the position of cupbearer to the king. Nehemiah received a delegation of visitors from Jerusalem and was given devastating news of the poverty and destruction there. He "sat down and wept, and mourned for many days; and fasting and praying before the God of heaven" (Nehemiah 1:4, NKJV.) His heart was broken with the plight of his countrymen and of his beloved city.

God miraculously answered Nehemiah's prayer. He moved the heart of the king and gave Nehemiah great favor. Nehemiah was allowed to return to his homeland and rebuild the walls of Jerusalem.

The New Testament is rife with instances of prayer petitions answered and people delivered—Peter from prison, John the Revelator from death on the Isle of Patmos, Paul from drowning at sea. Paul's ringing declaration while being tossed to and fro on the ship resonates:

> "For there stood by me this night an angel of the God to
> whom I belong and whom I serve" (Acts 27:23, NKJV.)

It is never too late for God to come to the aid of His children, and prayer is the means by which we touch Him. Israel is the key to America's survival—and prayer is the hand that turns the key.

CHAPTER 18

BLESSING BEGETS BLESSING

"In the last days the mountain of the LORD's temple will be established as chief among the mountains; it will be raised above the hills, and all nations will stream to it. Many peoples will come and say, 'Come, let us go up to the mountain of the LORD, to the house of the God of Jacob. He will teach us his ways, so that we may walk in his paths.' The law will go out from Zion, the word of the LORD from Jerusalem. He will judge between the nations and will settle disputes for many peoples. They will beat their swords into plowshares and their spears into pruning hooks. Nation will not take up sword against nation, nor will they train for war anymore."

ISAIAH 2:2-4, NIV

The Old and New Testaments are filled with scriptures about blessings. Genesis tells the stories of Abraham, Sarah, Isaac, Jacob, Moses, and a myriad of people who were blessed by Jehovah. The Apostle Paul began many of his letters to the various churches with a word of blessing.

God's blessings come to us in many ways. Too often we think in terms of material advantages, but that is not always the case as we can see in Deuteronomy 28. When God gives us a task to do, He will bless our attempts to accomplish His will:

175

Faithful is He who calls you, and He also will bring it to
pass, (I Thessalonians 5:2, NASB.)

During the first Persian Gulf War, Israel had not been allowed to join
the coalition because anti-Semitic Arab countries were screaming objec-
tions. President George H.W. Bush had also asked Israel not to retaliate when
bombarded by thirty-eight SCUD missile attacks; his request was honored.
Israel's reward for compliance was a $10 billion dollar loan guarantee freeze.
That money was desperately needed to provide housing for refugees, many
of them Russian Jews.

Once again the enemies of Israel had been appeased as its leaders were
hauled to Madrid and forced to give up land for peace—a peace that is yet
to come. Syria alone was given one billion dollars by the U.S. It was spent
on the purchase of North Korean missiles to be used against Israel. Many of
those missiles made their way to Lebanon and into the hands of Hezbollah,
the Iranian terror proxy. Those missiles, too, have targeted cities in Israel.

As President George H. W. Bush was opening the conference at the
Royal Palace in Madrid, the "Perfect Storm" (made famous in the movie)
developed in the north Atlantic creating the largest waves ever recorded in
that region. The storm traveled 1,000 miles "east to west" (as opposed to the
normal west to east pattern) to crash into the eastern coast of the United
States; thirty-five foot waves smashed into the Kennebunkport Maine home
of President Bush.

This was one of the worst storms in American history and one of the
top ten in insurance claims. When the Madrid Conference was moved to
Washington, D.C., for a resumption of the land-for-peace talks, Hurricane
Andrew struck Florida wreaking havoc and causing an estimated $30 billion
in damages. Some 180,000 Americans were left homeless. Andrew secured a
spot on the top-ten list of largest disasters in American history.

Failure or refusal to support the Jews and their right to return to their
ancient homeland places us in danger of being cursed by our Creator. God
Himself warns humanity of this danger:

And the one who curses you, I will curse" (Genesis12:3, NASB.)

By contesting the right of Jews to live in their covenant land, and thereby going against God's holy Word, many are opening themselves up to be cursed! The sad fact is that many governments, international organizations, Islamic groups and even some Christians do not acknowledge that divine right. For Christians, this unbiblical stand weakens our testimony, weakens the nation of Israel, weakens America, and puts the souls of our nation in harm's way.

Therefore, anyone who seeks the blessings bestowed by our Heavenly Father should make sure they are obeying His command to bless His special covenant people.

How can we secure the blessings of God? A number of ways have been outlined in *The Commanded Blessing*, but one of the most important is to support the God-given right of the Jewish people to live in their ancient homeland, especially pursuing their claim to Jerusalem.

God not only promised to reward individuals for blessing His covenant Jewish people, but He also pledged in the same Scripture to bless families, and by extension, entire nations:

> "And in you all the families of the earth shall be blessed,"
> (Genesis 12:3, NKJV.)

So the great Master of the Universe reveals that our personal, family, and national welfare is closely related to how we treat the called-out Jewish people. Should anyone need any other reason to support the contemporary offspring of Abraham, Isaac, and Jacob, especially in their brave endeavors to establish a thriving modern state within their biblically-designated ancestral borders? As we have seen, both the Old and New Testaments make abundantly clear that Christians must support Israel in every possible way. This does not mean that the Israeli people and their government are perfect; far from it. They are fallen human beings like everyone else on Earth, in desperate need of salvation. But the biblical prophets, including the Apostle Paul, foretold that the restored Jewish remnant in the Lord's land would mourn over their sins in the Last Days and be grafted back into their own sacred tree.

While waiting, working, and praying for "all Israel to be saved," we must wholeheartedly support what the sovereign Lord is doing in returning His ancient covenant people back to their God-given land. In doing so, we will be blessed as they are blessed. And best of all, we will make our eternal Father happy by obeying His revealed will on a matter that is clearly close to His heart.

America has been blessed because she has blessed the nation of Israel (Genesis 12:1-3). But America is in danger of moving away from the place of blessing to the place of cursing. The land-for-peace deals of recent years have placed Israel and the Jewish people in grave danger. To weaken Israel is to risk the peace of the world, for the road to world peace runs through Israel. Israel is the firewall between America and the anti-Semitic Islamic nations. America's ability to win the war on terrorism will be directly related to America's willingness to support Israel in winning the war against terrorism. Israel is the only power that restrains Islamic terrorism from the West. Jews are dying so that Christians can live. Terrorists consider America a Christian nation. They do not hate America because of Israel; they hate Israel because of America. They refer to America as the Great Satan, and Israel as the Little Satan.

Some may say, "I don't need to reach out to the House of Israel. Why, the Bible says there will be 'wars and rumors of wars' over there until the Messiah comes. It's all part of prophecy." This scripture from Matthew 24:6 refers to the entire world. As a matter of fact, there have only been approximately 268 years of peace on this planet in the last 6,000 years. This is despite the fact that some 8,000 peace treaties have been signed. Conversely, there have also been some amazing revivals during that time!

To simply say there is no need to support the Jewish people, my friend, is anti-Semitic nonsense. It is to say to Nehemiah, Esther and even our Lord that they were wrong to pray and reach out in love to the House of Israel. There are hundreds of examples of prophets, priests and kings who chose to light a candle in support of God's Chosen People rather than curse the darkness. Jesus is our perfect example. He fed the hungry; He gave water to the thirsty; He healed the sick.

Many use II Timothy 3:1 as an excuse to stand by and do nothing to aid Israel:

> "But know this, that in the last days perilous times will come." Matthew 24:6-8: "And you will hear of wars and rumors of wars. See that you are not troubled; for all these things must come to pass, but the end is not yet. For nation will rise against nation, and kingdom against kingdom. And there will be famines, pestilences, and earthquakes in various places. All these are the beginning of sorrows."

If we feel we are to do nothing for the Jewish people, then why do we do everything in our power to help hurting people in our own country?

Let me assure you today that God is not finished with the House of Israel and the Jewish people. The Church has not replaced Israel in the world today, and this false teaching is simply a tool of anti-Semites wielded against the Jews. It has been used to promote such abominable acts as the Spanish Inquisition, the Crusades, the pogroms in Russia, and the horrendous slaughter of the innocents during the Holocaust. These monstrous acts were done by men and women who professed to be "Christians."

Books filled with falsehoods, such as *The Protocols of the Learned Elders of Zion*, were introduced as a means to incite Jew-haters worldwide, and are still used today in Arab countries to justify attacks against Israel and Jews everywhere.

Theologian Charles Haddon Spurgeon said of this demonic doctrine:

> This false teaching of rejection of the Jews among Christians by scripture-ignorant pastors and leaders is merely a lame theological excuse to those who actually are at heart anti-Semitic. This very same attitude and mistaken belief gave rise to the horrors of the Crusades, the monstrous Inquisition, and the outright murder of innocents during the Pogroms, in which hundreds of thousands of Jewish

men, women, and children were slaughtered by people who regularly attended institutional "Christian" churches.

"I think we do not attach sufficient importance to the restoration of the Jews. We do not think enough of it. But certainly, if there is anything promised in the Bible, it is this.

"The day shall yet come when the Jews, who were the first Apostles to the Gentiles, the first missionaries to us, who were far off, shall be gathered in again. Until that shall be, the fullness of the Church's glory can never come. Matchless benefits to the world are bound up with the restoration of Israel; their gathering in shall be as life from the dead."[47]

All we need to do to understand the importance of supporting Israel and the Jewish people is to read Isaiah, Jeremiah, Ezekiel, Romans, and Ephesians to see that this land and these people are chosen of Jehovah God. In his book, *The Blessed Life*, Pastor Robert Morris says:

> Israel is smaller than the U.S. state of Rhode Island, and God chose tiny Israel for this reason. He knew that if the smallest could become the strongest, then the rest of the world would know that their God is the true God....Satan understands the plan and that is why he has tried to convince the Church to hate Jews for hundreds of years. [48]

This is one reason the Jerusalem Prayer Team has taken up the banner to protect and defend Eretz Yisrael until our Lord returns. We are honored to be able to stand with the Jewish people and to receive God's commanded blessing.

SCRIPTURES ON THE BLESSINGS OF GOD

Genesis 12:2 (KJV)
"And I will make of thee a great nation, and I will **bless** thee, and make thy name great; and thou shalt be a **blessing:**"

Genesis 22:15-18 (NIV)
The angel of the LORD called to Abraham from heaven a second time and said, "I swear by myself, declares the LORD, that because you have done this and have not withheld your son, your only son, I will surely **bless** you and make your descendants as numerous as the stars in the sky and as the sand on the seashore. Your descendants will take possession of the cities of their enemies, and through your offspring all nations on earth will be **blessed**, because you have obeyed me."

Genesis 28:4 (NIV)
May he give you and your descendants the **blessing** given to Abraham, so that you may take possession of the land where you now live as an alien, the land God gave to Abraham."

Genesis 28:18 (NIV)
Your descendants will be like the dust of the earth, and you will spread out to the west and to the east, to the north and to the south. All peoples on earth will be **blessed** through you and your offspring.

Genesis 39:5 (NIV)
From the time he put him in charge of his household and of all that he owned, the LORD **blessed** the household of the Egyptian because of Joseph. The **blessing** of the LORD was on everything Potiphar had, both in the house and in the field.

Genesis 49:22-26 (NIV)
"Joseph is a fruitful vine, a fruitful vine near a spring, whose branches climb over a wall. With bitterness archers attacked him; they shot at him with hostility. But his bow remained steady, his strong arms stayed limber, because of the hand of the Mighty One of Jacob, because of the Shepherd, the Rock of Israel, because of your father's God, who helps you, because of the Almighty, who **blesses** you with **blessings** of the skies above, **blessings** of the deep springs below, **blessings** of the breast and womb. Your father's **blessings** are greater than the **blessings** of the ancient mountains, than the bounty of the age-old hills.

Exodus 23:25 (NIV)

Worship the LORD your God, and his **blessing** will be on your food and water. I will take away sickness from among you…,

Leviticus 25:21 (NIV)

I will send you such a **blessing** in the sixth year that the land will yield enough for three years.

Numbers 23:20 (NIV)

I have received a command to **bless**; he has **blessed**, and I cannot change it.

Numbers 6:24-26 (NIV)

"The LORD **bless** you and keep you;the LORD make his face shine upon you and be gracious to you; the LORD turn his face toward you and give you peace."

Deuteronomy 7:9 (NASB)

"Know therefore that the LORD your God, He is God, the faithful God, who keeps His covenant and His lovingkindness to a thousandth generation with those who love Him and keep His commandments;"

Deuteronomy 7:12-15 (NIV)

If you pay attention to these laws and are careful to follow them, then the LORD your God will keep his covenant of love with you, as he swore to your forefathers. He will love you and **bless** you and increase your numbers. He will **bless** the fruit of your womb, the crops of your land—your grain, new wine and oil—the calves of your herds and the lambs of your flocks in the land that he swore to your forefathers to give you. You will be **blessed** more than any other people; none of your men or women will be childless, nor any of your livestock without young. The LORD will keep you free from every disease.

Deuteronomy 11:27 (KJV)

"A **blessing**, if ye obey the commandments of the LORD your God, which I command you this day."

Deuteronomy 15:5 (NLT)

You will receive this **blessing** if you are careful to obey all the commands of the LORD your God that I am giving you today.

Deuteronomy 28:1-12 (NIV)

If you fully obey the LORD your God and carefully follow all his commands I give you today, the LORD your God will set you high above all the nations on earth. All these **blessings** will come upon you and accompany you if you obey the LORD your God: You will be **blessed** in the city and **blessed** in the country. The fruit of your womb will be **blessed**, and the crops of your land and the young of your livestock—the calves of your herds and the lambs of your flocks. Your basket and your kneading trough will be **blessed**. You will be **blessed** when you come in and **blessed** when you go out. The LORD will grant that the enemies who rise up against you will be defeated before you. They will come at you from one direction but flee from you in seven. The LORD will send a **blessing** on your barns and on everything you put your hand to. The LORD your God will **bless** you in the land he is giving you. The LORD will establish you as his holy people, as he promised you on oath, if you keep the commands of the LORD your God and walk in his ways. Then all the peoples on earth will see that you are called by the name of the LORD, and they will fear you. The LORD will grant you abundant prosperity—in the fruit of your womb, the young of your livestock and the crops of your ground—in the land he swore to your forefathers to give you. The LORD will open the heavens, the storehouse of his bounty, to send rain on your land in season and to **bless** all the work of your hands. You will lend to many nations but will borrow from none. The LORD will make you the head, not the tail. If you pay attention to the commands of the LORD your God that I give you this day and carefully follow them, you will always be at the top, never at the bottom. 14 Do not turn aside from any of the commands I give you today, to the right or to the left, following other gods and serving them.

1 Kings 8:56-61 (NIV)

Praise be to the LORD, who has given rest to his people Israel just as he promised. Not one word has failed of all the good promises he gave through his servant Moses. May the LORD our God be with us as he was with our fathers; may he never leave us nor forsake us. May he turn our hearts to him, to walk in all his ways and to keep the commands, decrees and regulations he gave our fathers. And may these words of mine, which I have prayed before the LORD, be near to the LORD our God day and night, that he may uphold the cause of his servant and the cause of his people Israel according to each day's need, so that all the peoples of the earth may know that the LORD is God and that there is no other. But your hearts must be fully committed to the LORD our God, to live by his decrees and obey his commands, as at this time."

Nehemiah 9:5 (NIV)

…"Stand up and praise the LORD your God, who is from everlasting to everlasting." "**Blessed** be your glorious name, and may it be exalted above all **blessing** and praise.

Job 5:17 (NIV)

"**Blessed** is the one whom God corrects; so do not despise the discipline of the Almighty.

Psalm 1:1 (NIV)

Blessed is the man who does not walk in the counsel of the wicked or stand in the way of sinners or sit in the seat of mockers.

Psalm 3:8 (NIV)

From the LORD comes deliverance. May your **blessing** be on your people. Selah

Psalm 21:4 (NIV)

You came to greet him with rich **blessings** and placed a crown of pure gold on his head.

Psalms 24:3-5 (NASB)

"Who may ascend into the hill of the LORD?
And who may stand in His holy place?
He who has clean hands and a pure heart,
Who has not lifted up his soul to falsehood
And has not sworn deceitfully.
He shall receive a **blessing** from the LORD
And righteousness from the God of his salvation."

Psalm 33:12 (NIV)

Blessed is the nation whose God is the LORD, the people he chose for his inheritance.

Psalm 34:8 (NIV)

Taste and see that the LORD is good; **blessed** is the one who takes refuge in him.

Psalm 40:4 (NIV)

Blessed is the one who trusts in the LORD, who does not look to the proud, to those who turn aside to false gods.

Psalm 67:1-2 (NIV)

May God be gracious to us and **bless** us and make his face shine upon us, that your ways may be known on earth, your salvation among all nations.

Psalm 84:12 (NIV)

LORD Almighty, **blessed** is the one who trusts in you.

Psalm 89:15 (NIV)

Blessed are those who have learned to acclaim you, who walk in the light of your presence, LORD.

Psalm 106:3 (NIV)
    Blessed are those who act justly, who always do what is right.

Psalm 133:3 (NIV)
    It is as if the dew of Hermon were falling on Mount Zion. For there the LORD bestows his **blessing**, even life forevermore.

Proverbs 3:13 (NIV)
    Blessed are those who find wisdom, those who gain understanding,

Proverbs 3:33 (NIV)
    The curse of the LORD *is* on the house of the wicked, But He **blesses** the home of the just.

Proverbs 10:6-7 (NIV)
    Blessings crown the head of the righteous, but violence overwhelms the mouth of the wicked. The memory of the righteous will be a **blessing**, but the name of the wicked will rot.

Proverbs 10:22 (NASB)
    "It is the **blessing** of the LORD that makes rich, And He adds no sorrow to it."

Proverbs 11:11 (NIV)
    Through the **blessing** of the upright a city is exalted, but by the mouth of the wicked it is destroyed.

Proverbs 16:20 (NIV)
    Whoever gives heed to instruction prospers, and **blessed** is the one who trusts in the LORD.

Proverbs 28:20 (NKJV)
    A faithful man will abound with **blessings**, But he who hastens to be rich will not go unpunished.

Proverbs 24:25 (NKJV)
    But those who rebuke *the wicked* will have delight, And a good **blessing** will come upon them.

Isaiah 44:3 (NIV)
    For I will pour water on the thirsty land, and streams on the dry ground; I will pour out my Spirit on your offspring, and my **blessing** on your descendants.

Jeremiah 17:7 (NIV)
    "But **blessed** is the one who trusts in the LORD, whose confidence is in him.

Ezekiel 34:26 (NIV)

I will **bless** them and the places surrounding my hill. I will send down showers in season; there will be showers of **blessing**.

Ezekiel 44:30 (NIV)

The best of all the firstfruits and of all your special gifts will belong to the priests. You are to give them the first portion of your ground meal so that a **blessing** may rest on your household.

Joel 2:14 (NIV)

Who knows? He may turn and have pity and leave behind a **blessing**, grain offerings and drink offerings for the LORD your God.

Malachi 3:10 (KJV)

"Bring ye all the tithes into the storehouse, that there may be meat in mine house, and prove me now herewith, saith the LORD of hosts, if I will not open you the windows of heaven, and pour you out a **blessing**, that there shall not be room enough to receive it."

Matthew 5:2-12 (NIV)

"**Blessed** are the poor in spirit,
for theirs is the kingdom of heaven.
Blessed are those who mourn,
for they will be comforted.
Blessed are the meek,
for they will inherit the earth.
Blessed are those who hunger and thirst for righteousness,
for they will be filled.
Blessed are the merciful,
for they will be shown mercy.
Blessed are the pure in heart,
for they will see God.
Blessed are the peacemakers,
for they will be called sons of God.
Blessed are those who are persecuted because of righteousness,
for theirs is the kingdom of heaven.
"**Blessed** are you when people insult you, persecute you and falsely say all kinds of evil against you because of me. Rejoice and be glad, because great is your reward in heaven, for in the same way they persecuted the prophets who were before you.

Luke 11:28 (NIV)

He replied, "**Blessed** rather are those who hear the word of God and obey it."

John 1:16 (NIV)
From the fullness of his grace we have all received one **blessing** after another.

Romans 4:7 (NIV)
"**Blessed** are those whose transgressions are forgiven, whose sins are covered.

Ephesians 1:3 (NIV)
Praise be to the God and Father of our Lord Jesus Christ, who has **blessed** us in the heavenly realms with every spiritual **blessing** in Christ.

Philippians 4:19 (KJV)
"But my God shall supply all your need according to his riches in glory by Christ Jesus."

Hebrews 6:7 (NIV)
Land that drinks in the rain often falling on it and that produces a crop useful to those for whom it is farmed receives the **blessing** of God.

Hebrew 6:14 (NKJV)
"Surely **blessing** I will **bless** you, and multiplying I will multiply you."*

James 1:12 (NIV)
Blessed is the man who perseveres under trial, because when he has stood the test, he will receive the crown of life that God has promised to those who love him.

1 Peter 3:9 (NIV)
Do not repay evil with evil or insult with insult, but with **blessing**, because to this you were called so that you may inherit a **blessing**.

ENDNOTES

1. *Vine* et al., Vol. 1, s.v. "Together," 263.

2. "Transfiguration," Bible Encyclopedia, http://bibleencyclopedia.com/transfiguration. htm; accessed May 2013.

3. Devotional Reflections from the Bible, http://www.devotional-reflections-from-the-bible.com/Psalm133.html; accessed May 2013.

4. Johnny Jones, "Commanded Blessing," http://sozotoday.com/?p=1525; accessed May 2013.

5. Abraham, Jewish Virtual Library, http://www.jewishvirtuallibrary.org/jsource/biography/abraham.html; accessed July 2012.

6. "Abraham, Sarah, and Hagar: A Family Affair," Project Genesis, Inc., 1996, http://www.torah.org/projects/genesis/topic6.html; accessed May 2013.

7. C. H. Spurgeon, "The Obedience of Faith," August 2, 1890, at the Metropolitan Tabernacle, Newington.

8. Jim Hearst and Tim Finley, "Ruth: Romance and Redemption," Grace Communion International, Edited in 2012, http://www.gci.org/bible/hist/ruth3; accessed May 2013.

9. Carolyn Custis James, *The Gospel of Ruth: Loving God Enough to Break the Rules* (Grand Rapids, MI: Zondervan, 2008), pp. 162-163.

10. http://hesed.com/hesed.html; accessed June 2013.

11. (*Sermons on Bible Subjects,* E.P. Dutton & Company, London, 1906, p. 78).

12. Charles Swindoll, *Elijah: A Man of Heroism and Humility* (Nashville, TN: Word Publishing, 2000), p. 9.

13. Merriam-Webster, http://www.merriam-webster.com/; accessed August 2012.

14. Matt Barber, "Today's Baal Worshippers," *World Net Daily,* December 19, 2008, http://www.wnd.com/2008/12/83960/; accessed August 2012.

15. http://www.oralroberts.com/wordpress/wp-content/uploads/DOC_BIN/miracles_mag/2010/pdf/miraclesV3N3.pdf; accessed May 2013.

16. Arthur Smith, "The Fourth Man," http://artists.letssingit.com/statler-brothers-lyrics-the-fourth-man-3z8kkmf#ixzz20uloRyUR, accessed July 2012.

17. Frank Wallace, "Daniel's Prayer Life," BibleCentre.org, http://biblecentre.org/
     addresses/fw_prayer_daniel.htm; accessed June 2013.

18. Charles Swindoll, Come before Winter and Share my Hope (Portland, OR:
     Multnomah Press, 1985), p.187.

19. John MacArthur, Jr., *The MacArthur New Testament Commentary* (Chicago: Moody
     Publishers, 1983–2007). Quoted from a sermon by Rev. Dave Schmidt, Southside
     Church of Christ, Fort Myer, FL; http://www.southsidechurchofchrist.com/sermons/
     the-faith-of-abel.html; accessed June 2012.

20. Juliane von Mittelstaedt, Christoph Schult, Daniel Steinvorth, Thilo Thielke,
     Volkhard Windfuhr, "Christianity's Modern-Day Martyrs: Victims of Radical Islam,"
     ABC News, March 1, 2010, http://abcnews.go.com/International/christian-martyrs-
     victims-radical-islam/story?id=9976549; accessed September 2012.

21. Personal Interview with Mordechai Gur, 1995.

22. *Ibid.*

23. Personal interview with Chief Rabbi Shlomo Goren, 1995.

24. *Ibid.*

25. Evans, Mike D., *Save Jerusalem*, (Euless, TX: Bedford Books, 1995), p. 94.

26. Fuel for Truth; http://www.fuelfortruth.org/thetruth/truth_10.asp; accessed April
     2010.

27. Moshe Dayan, Address in the General Assembly by Foreign Minister Dayan,
     September 27, 1979; http://www.mfa.gov.il/MFA/Foreign%20Relations/Israels%20
     Foreign%20Relations%20since%201947/1979-1980/46%20Address%20in%20the%20
     General%20Assembly%20by%20Foreign%20Mini; accessed April 2010.

28. Wise, Christopher, *Derrida, Africa and the Middle East* (New York, NY: St. Martin's
     Press, 2009), p. 59.

29. Misselwitz, Philip and Rieniets, Tim, City of Collision: Jerusalem and the Principles
     of Conflict Urbanism; (Germany: Die Deutsche Bibliothek, 2006), p. 49.

30. Kollek, Teddy and Pearlman, Moshe (Israel: Steimatzky Group, 1987)

31. Psalm 122:6, Biblecommentary.com, http://www.biblestudytools.com/commentaries/
     treasury-of-david/psalms-122-6.html; accessed June 2013.

32. Irwin N. Graulich, "Why America Supports Israel," *FrontPageMag.com*, December
     20, 2002; http://archive.frontpagemag.com/readArticle.aspx?ARTID=20579; accessed
     January 2012.

33. Paul Goldman, "Dying 4-year old girl finds life-savers in the land of the enemy,"

http://worldnews.nbcnews.com/_news/2013/05/26/18445610-dying-4-year-old-girl-finds-life-savers-in-land-of-the-enemy?lite, May 2013; accessed June 2013.

34. Marcella Rosen, "65 years of innovations from Israel," May 9, 2013, *The Jewish Observer,* http://jewishobservernashville.org/2013/05/09/65-years-of-innovations-from-israel/; accessed June 2013.

35. See the full list of innovations and inventions at http://jewishobservernashville.org/2013/05/09/65-years-of-innovations-from-israel/.

36. "Nobel Prize in Literature 2002," Nobel Foundation; accessed June 2013.

37. "The Nobel Peace Prize for 1986: Elie Wiesel," Nobelprize.org, 14 October 1986; accessed June 2013.

38. "Professor Robert Aumann: He's Got Game," *Jerusalem Post, November 1, 2005,* www.jpost.com/servlet/Satellite?cid=1129540643006&pagename=JPost%2FJPArticle%2FShowFull; accessed June 2013.

39. Robert Aumann, http://en.wikipedia.org/wiki/Robert_Aumann, accessed June 2013.

40. http://www.quotationcollection.com/author/Ernest-Hemingway/quotes; accessed June 2013.

41. L'Osservatore Romano, Vatican Daily, 20 April 1984.

42. Seymour M. Hersh, *The Samson Option: Israel's Nuclear Arsenal and American Foreign Policy* (New York: Vintage Books, 1991), p. 223.

43. Seymour M. Hersh, *The Price of Power: Kissinger in the Nixon White House* (New York: Summit Books, 1983), p. 234.

44. Mandy Katz, "Do We Divide the Holiest Holy City?", *Moment Magazine,* May 8, 2012, http://www.momentmag.com/do-we-divide-the-holiest-holy-city/; accessed June 2013

45. Sennacherib. (n.d.). *Easton's 1897 Bible Dictionary.* Retrieved June 25, 2013, from Dictionary.com website: http://dictionary.reference.com/browse/Sennacherib; accessed June 2013.

46. Israel Matzav, "I will bless those who bless you, and I will curse him that curses you," Thursday, April 22, 2010, http://israelmatzav.blogspot.com/search?q=I+will+bless+them+that+bless+you; accessed June 2013.

47. Charles Haddon Spurgeon, "The Restoration and Conversion of the Jews," Vol. 1 pg. 214, Vol. 17 pp. 703,704, accessed June 2013 from http://israelsmessiah.com/religions/christianity/christians_for_jews.htm.

48. Robert Morris, *The Blessed Life* (Ventura, CA: Regal, 2004), pp. 207-208.

BOOKS BY: MIKE EVANS

Israel: America's Key to Survival

Save Jerusalem

The Return

Jerusalem D.C.

Purity and Peace of Mind

Who Cries for the Hurting?

Living Fear Free

I Shall Not Want

Let My People Go

Jerusalem Betrayed

Seven Years of Shaking: A Vision

The Nuclear Bomb of Islam

Jerusalem Prophecies

Pray For Peace of Jerusalem

America's War: The Beginning
of the End

The Jerusalem Scroll

The Prayer of David

The Unanswered Prayers of Jesus

God Wrestling

Why Christians Should Support Israel

The American Prophecies

Beyond Iraq: The Next Move

The Final Move beyond Iraq

Showdown with Nuclear Iran

Jimmy Carter: The Liberal Left and
World Chaos

Atomic Iran

Cursed

Betrayed

The Light

Corrie's Reflections & Meditations
(booklet)

GAMECHANGER SERIES:
GameChanger
Samson Option
The Four Horsemen

THE PROTOCOLS SERIES:
The Protocols
The Candidate

The Revolution

The Final Generation

Seven Days

The Locket

Living in the F.O.G.

Persia: The Final Jihad

Jerusalem

The History of Christian Zionism

Countdown

Ten Boom

The Commanded Blessing

COMING SOON:

Born Again: Israel's Rebirth

Presidents in Prophecy

To purchase, contact: orders@timeworthybooks.com
P. O. Box 30000, Phoenix, AZ 85046